CBSE Term II
2022

Informatics Practices

Class XI

CBSE Term II 2022

Informatics Practices

Class XI

- Complete Theory Covering NCERT
- Case Based Questions
- Short/Long Answer Type Questions
- 3 Practice Papers with Explanations

Author
Sanjib Pal

ARIHANT PRAKASHAN (School Division Series)

CBSE Term II
2022

ARIHANT PRAKASHAN (School Division Series)

ॐ **Administrative & Production Offices**

Regd. Office
'Ramchhaya' 4577/15, Agarwal Road, Darya Ganj, New Delhi -110002
Tele: 011- 47630600, 43518550

ॐ **Head Office**
Kalindi, TP Nagar, Meerut (UP) - 250002, Tel: 0121-7156203, 7156204

ॐ **Sales & Support Offices**
Agra, Ahmedabad, Bengaluru, Bareilly, Chennai, Delhi, Guwahati, Hyderabad, Jaipur, Jhansi, Kolkata, Lucknow, Nagpur & Pune.

ॐ **ISBN :** 978-93-25796-88-1

ॐ **PRICE :** ₹125.00

PO No : TXT-XX-XXXXXXX-X-XX

Published by Arihant Publications (India) Ltd.

For further information about the books published by Arihant, log on to www.arihantbooks.com or e-mail at info@arihantbooks.com

Follow us on   

Contents

Watch Free Learning Videos

Subscribe **arihant** You Tube Channel

☑ Video Solutions of CBSE Sample Papers
☑ Chapterwise Important MCQs
☑ CBSE Updates

Syllabus

CBSE Term II Class XI

Informatics Practices

		Marks
3.	Database concepts and the Structured Query Language	30
4.	Introduction to Emerging Trends	05
	Total	**35**

UNIT 3 : Database concepts and the Structured Query Language

- Database Concepts: Introduction to database concepts and its need, Database Management System. Relational data model: concept of attribute, domain, tuple, relation, candidate key, primary key, alternate key, foreign key.

- Structured Query Language: Data Definition Language, Data Query Language and Data Manipulation Language, Introduction to MySQL: Creating a database, using database, showing tables using MySQL.

- Data Types : char, varchar, int, float, date.

- Data Definition Commands: CREATE, DROP, ALTER (Add and Remove primary key, attribute). Data Query Commands: SELECT-FROM- WHERE, LIKE, BETWEEN, IN, ORDER BY, using arithmetic, logical, relational operators and NULL values in queries, Distinct clause Data Manipulation Commands: INSERT, UPDATE, DELETE.

UNIT 4 : Introduction to the Emerging Trends

- Artificial Intelligence, Machine Learning, Natural Language Processing,
- mmersive experience (AR, VR), Robotics
- Big data and its characteristics, Internet of Things (IoT), Sensors, Smart cities,
- Cloud Computing and Cloud Services (SaaS, IaaS, PaaS);
- Grid Computing, Block chain technology.

CBSE Circular

Acad – 51/2021, 05 July 2021

Exam Scheme Term I & II

केन्द्रीय माध्यमिक शिक्षा बोर्ड

(शिक्षा मंत्रालय, भारत सरकार के अधीन एक स्वायत संगठन)

CENTRAL BOARD OF SECONDARY EDUCATION

(An Autonomous Organisation under the Ministryof Education, Govt. of India)

CBSE/DIR (ACAD)/2021

Date: July 05, 2021
Circular No: Acad-51/2021

All the Heads of Schools affiliated to CBSE

Subject: Special Scheme of Assessment for Board Examination Classes X and XII for the Session 2021-22

COVID 19 pandemic caused almost all CBSE schools to function in a virtual mode for most part of the academic session of 2020-21. Due to the extreme risk associated with the conduct of Board examinations during the second wave in April 2021, CBSE had to cancel both its class X and XII Board examinations of the year 2021 and results are to be declared on the basis of a credible, reliable, flexible and valid alternative assessment policy. This, in turn, also necessitated deliberations over alternative ways to look at the learning objectives as well as the conduct of the Board Examinations for the academic session 2021-22 in case the situation remains unfeasible.

CBSE has also held stake holder consultations with Government schools as well as private independent schools from across the country especially schools from the remote rural areas and a majority of them have requested for the rationalization of the syllabus, similar to last year in view of reduced time permitted for organizing online classes. The Board has also considered the concerns regarding differential availability of electronic gadgets, connectivity and effectiveness of online teaching and other socio-economic issues specially with respect to students from economically weaker section and those residing in far flung areas of the country. In a survey conducted by CBSE, it was revealed that the rationalized syllabus notified for the session 2020-21 was effective for schools in covering the syllabus and helped learners in achieving learning objectives in a less stressful manner.

In the above backdrop and in line with the Board's continued focus on assessing stipulated learning outcomes by making the examinations competencies and core concepts based, student-centric, transparent, technology-driven, and having advance provision of alternatives for different future scenarios, the following schemes are introduced for the Academic Session for Class X and Class XII 2021-22.

केन्द्रीय माध्यमिक शिक्षा बोर्ड

(शिक्षा मंत्रालय, भारत सरकार के अधीन एक स्वायत संगठन)

CENTRAL BOARD OF SECONDARY EDUCATION

(An Autonomous Organisation under the Ministryof Education, Govt. of India)

Special Scheme for 2021-22

A. Academic session to be divided into 2 Terms with approximately 50% syllabus in each term:

The syllabus for the Academic session 2021-22 will be divided into 2 terms by following a systematic approach by looking into the interconnectivity of concepts and topics by the Subject Experts and the Board will conduct examinations at the end of each term on the basis of the bifurcated syllabus. This is done to increase the probability of having a Board conducted classes X and XII examinations at the end of the academic session.

B. The syllabus for the Board examination 2021-22 will be rationalized similar to that of the last academic session to be notified in July 2021. For academic transactions, however, schools will follow the curriculum and syllabus released by the Board vide Circular no. F.1001/CBSE-Acad/Curriculum/2021 dated 31 March 2021. Schools will also use alternative academic calendar and inputs from the NCERT on transacting the curriculum.

C. Efforts will be made to make Internal Assessment/ Practical/ Project work more credible and valid as per the guidelines and Moderation Policy to be announced by the Board to ensure fair distribution of marks.

Details of Curriculum Transaction

- Schools will continue teaching in distance mode till the authorities permit in-person mode of teaching in schools.

- **Classes IX-X: Internal Assessment** (throughout the year-irrespective of Term I and II) would include the *3 periodic tests, student enrichment, portfolio and practical work/ speaking listening activities/ project*.

- **Classes XI-XII: Internal Assessment** (throughout the year-irrespective of Term I and II) would include end of topic or unit tests/ exploratory activities/ practicals/ projects.

- Schools would create a student profile for all assessment undertaken over the year and retain the evidences in digital format.

- CBSE will facilitate schools to upload marks of Internal Assessment on the CBSE IT platform.

- Guidelines for Internal Assessment for all subjects will also be released along with the rationalized term wise divided syllabus for the session 2021-22.The Board would also provide additional resources like sample assessments, question banks, teacher training etc. for more reliable and valid internal assessments.

केन्द्रीय माध्यमिक शिक्षा बोर्ड

(शिक्षा मंत्रालय, भारत सरकार के अधीन एक स्वायत संगठन)

CENTRAL BOARD OF SECONDARY EDUCATION

(An Autonomous Organisation under the Ministryof Education, Govt. of India)

Term I Examinations:

- At the end of the first term, the Board will organize **Term I Examination** in a flexible schedule to be conducted between November-December 2021 with a window period of 4-8 weeks for schools situated in different parts of country and abroad. Dates for conduct of examinations will be notified subsequently.

- The Question Paper will have Multiple Choice Questions (MCQ) including case-based MCQs and MCQs on assertion-reasoning type. Duration of test will be **90 minutes** and it will cover only the rationalized syllabus of **Term I only** (i.e. approx. 50% of the entire syllabus).

- Question Papers will be sent by the CBSE to schools along with marking scheme.

- The exams will be conducted under the supervision of the External Center Superintendents and Observers appointed by CBSE.

- The responses of students will be captured on OMR sheets which, after scanning may be directly uploaded at CBSE portal or alternatively may be evaluated and marks obtained will be uploaded by the school on the very same day. The final direction in this regard will be conveyed to schools by the Examination Unit of the Board.

- Marks of the **Term I** Examination will contribute to the final overall score of students.

Term II Examination/ Year-end Examination:

- At the end of the second term, the Board would organize **Term II or Year-end Examination** based on the rationalized syllabus of Term II only (i.e. approximately 50% of the entire syllabus).

- This examination would be held around **March-April 2022** at the examination centres fixed by the Board.

- The paper will be of **2 hours duration** and have questions of different formats (case-based/ situation based, open ended- short answer/ long answer type).

- In case the situation is not conducive for normal descriptive examination **a 90 minute MCQ based exam** will be conducted at the end of the Term II also.

- Marks of the Term II Examination would contribute to the final overall score.

केन्द्रीय माध्यमिक शिक्षा बोर्ड

(शिक्षा मंत्रालय, भारत सरकार के अधीन एक स्वायत संगठन)

CENTRAL BOARD OF SECONDARY EDUCATION

(An Autonomous Organisation under the Ministryof Education, Govt. of India)

Assessment / Examination as per different situations

A. In case the situation of the pandemic improves and students are able to come to schools or centres for taking the exams.

Board would conduct Term I and Term II examinations at schools/centres and the theory marks will be distributed equally between the two exams.

B. In case the situation of the pandemic forces complete closure of schools during November-December 2021, but Term II exams are held at schools or centres.

Term I MCQ based examination would be done by students online/offline from home - in this case, the weightage of this exam for the final score would be reduced, and weightage of Term II exams will be increased for declaration of final result.

C. In case the situation of the pandemic forces complete closure of schools during March-April 2022, but Term I exams are held at schools or centres.

Results would be based on the performance of students on Term I MCQ based examination and internal assessments. The weightage of marks of Term I examination conducted by the Board will be increased to provide year end results of candidates.

D. In case the situation of the pandemic forces complete closure of schools and Board conducted Term I and II exams are taken by the candidates from home in the session 2021-22.

Results would be computed on the basis of the Internal Assessment/Practical/Project Work and Theory marks of Term-I and II exams taken by the candidate from home in Class X / XII subject to the moderation or other measures to ensure validity and reliability of the assessment.

In all the above cases, data analysis of marks of students will be undertaken to ensure the integrity of internal assessments and home based exams.

Dr. Joseph Emmanuel
Director (Academics)

CHAPTER 01

Database Concepts

In this Chapter...

- Database Management System (DBMS)
- Working of Databse
- View of Data (Data Abstraction)
- Data Models
- Relational Database
- Keys

A database can be defined as a collection of information organized in such a way that a computer program can be used to retrieve data quickly. You can think of a database as an electronic filing system.

The contents of a database are obtained by combining the data from all the different sources in an organization. This data forms the base for all further activities such as performing logical, mathematical and other operations and maintains any information that may be necessary to the decision-making processes involved in the management of that organization.

A database has the following properties

- It is a collection of data elements representing real-world information.
- It is logical, coherent and internally consistent.

For example, consider the names, telephone numbers and addresses of the relatives. You may have recorded this data in an indexed address book or you may have stored it on a hard drive, using application software such as Microsoft Access or Excel. This collection of related data with an implicit meaning is known as a **Database**.

Database Management System (DBMS)

A Database Management System is a software system that enables users to define, create and maintain the database and provides controlled access to this database.

The primary goal of a DBMS is to provide a way to store and retrieve database information that is both convenient and efficient. Data in a database can be added, deleted, changed, sorted or searched, all using a DBMS.

Application program accesses the data stored in the database by sending request to the DBMS. *For example,* MySQL, INGRES, MS-ACCESS etc.

The purpose of a Database Management System is to bridge the gap between information and data. The data stored in memory or on disk must be converted to usable information.

The basic processes that are supported by a DBMS are

(i) Specification of data types, structures and constraints to be considered in an application.
(ii) Storing the data itself into persistent storage.
(iii) Manipulation of the database.
(iv) Querying the database to retrieve desired information.
(v) Updating the content of the database.

Advantages of DBMS

(i) Reduced data redundancy
(ii) Elimination of inconsistency
(iii) Data sharing
(iv) Data integrity
(v) Data security
(vi) Backup and recovery

Limitations of DBMS

(i) High cost
(ii) Database failure
(iii) Data quality
(iv) Confidentiality, privacy and security

Need of Database System

The need of database systems arose in the early 1960s in response to the **traditional file processing system**. In the file processing system, the data is stored in the form of files, and a number of application programs are written by programmers to add, modify, delete, and retrieve data to and from appropriate files.

New application programs are added to the system as the need arises. *For example*, suppose a saving bank decides to offer current accounts. As a result, the bank creates new permanent files that contain information about all the current accounts maintained in the bank, and it may have to write new application programs to deal with situations that do not arise in saving accounts, such as overdrafts. Thus, as time goes by, the system acquires more files and more application programs.

However, the file processing system has a number of disadvantages, which are given below

- Some information may be duplicated in several files.
- The file processing system lacks the insulation between program and data.
- Handling new queries is difficult, since it requires change in the existing application programs or requires a new application program.
- In this system, all the integrity rules need to be explicitly programmed in all application programs, which are using that particular data item.
- This system lacks security features. To overcome these problems, database system was designed.

Components of Database System

A database system is composed of four components- User, Hardware, Software and Data, which coordinate with one another to form an effective database system.

The major components of a database system are described below

(i) **User** The users are the people who manage the database and perform different operations on it.

Basically, users are those persons who need the information from the database to carry out their primary business responsibilities i.e. personnel, staff, clerical etc.

There are mainly three kinds of people who plays different roles in database system. They are **application programmers**, who develop the application programs, the **end-users** access the database from a terminal using a query language provided by database system and **database administrator**, who is responsible for the design, construction and maintenance of a database system.

Database Administrator (DBA)

The person having the central control over the system is called Database Administrator. The DBA has many different responsibilities but the overall goal of a DBA is to maintain the database system and to provide users with access to the required information when they need it. The DBA makes sure that the database is protected.

Some responsibilities of DBA are as follows

- Ensuring regular and accurate update of the database.
- Identifying and resolving user's problem.
- Schema and physical organization modification.
- Storage structure and access method definition.
- Processing and maintaining database.

(ii) **Hardware** The hardware consists of various secondary storage devices, such as magnetic tapes, hard disks, floppy disks, CD-ROM's etc, on which data is stored and the input/output devices, such as mouse, keyboard, lightpen, printers, scanners etc., which are used for storing (by providing commands) and retrieving the required data in an efficient manner.

Since database can range from those of a single user with a desktop computer to those on mainframe computers with thousands of users, therefore proper care should be taken for choosing appropriate hardware devices for a required database.

(iii) **Software** This is the most important component of database. It acts as an interface between the user and the database. In other words, software interacts with the users, application programs, and database of a particular storage media to insert, update, delete and retrieve data.

For performing these operations such as insertion, deletion and updation we can either use the query languages like SQL, QUEL or application softwares such as Visual Basic, etc.

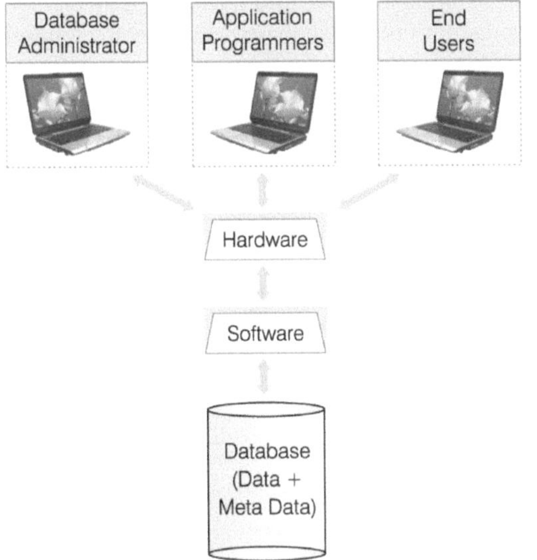

(iv) **Data** It is an important component of database.

Most of the organizations generate, store and process large amount of data. The data act as a bridge between the hardware, software and the users.

A database contains various types of data

- **User Data** It contains a table of data in the form of rows (records) and columns (fields).

- **Meta Data** It means 'data about data' i.e. a logical description of the structure of a data.

- **Application Data** It contains the structure and format queries, reports and other application components.

Working of Database

Databases are created to operate on large quantities of information by input, store, retrieve, and manage the information.

Database is a centralized location which provides an easy way to access the data by several users. It does not keep the separate copies of a particular data file still a number of users can access the same data at the same time.

As the below diagram shows, to perform any operation in the presence of a Database Management System (DBMS).

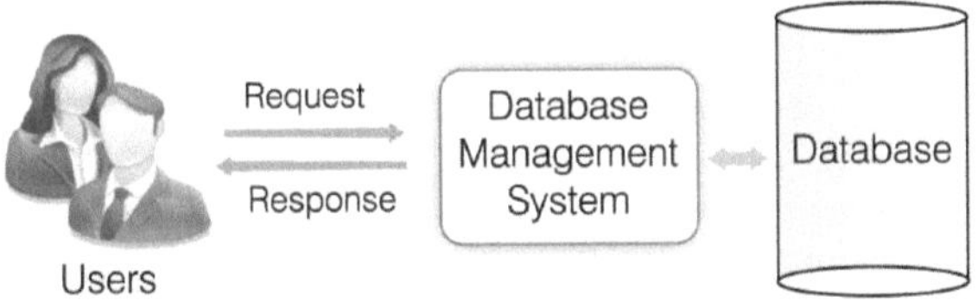

Here, DBMS works as an interface between the user and the centralized database. First, a request or query is forwarded to a DBMS which works (i.e., a searching process is started on the centralized database) on the received query with the available data and if the result is obtained, is forwarded to the user. If the output does not completely fulfill the requirements of the user then a rollback (again search) is done and again search process is performed until the desired output is obtained.

DBMS *versus* File Processing System

Database Management System	File Processing System
A database management system co-ordinates both the physical and the logical access to the data.	File processing system co-ordinates only the physical access.
A database management system is a bundle of applications, i.e. dedicated for managing data stored in a database.	A file processing system is a collection of raw data files stored in the hard drive of a system.
A database management system is designed to allow flexible access to data (i.e. queries).	File processing system is designed to allow predetermined access to data (i.e. compiled programs).
A database management system is designed to co-ordinate multiple users accessing the same data at the same time.	A file processing system is usually designed to allow one or more programs to access different data files at the same time.

View of Data (Data Abstraction)

The major purpose of a database system is to provide users with an abstract view of data. That is, the system hides certain details of how the data are stored and maintained.

For the system to be usable, it must retrieve data efficiently. The need for efficiency has led designers to use complex data structures to represent data in the database.

Since many database system users are not computer trained, developers hide the complexity from users through several levels of abstraction, to simplify user's interactions with the system. This concept is known as data abstraction.

Several levels of abstraction are described below

(i) **Internal Level** It is the lowest level of abstraction that describes how the data is physically stored and organised on storage medium. It describes complex low-level data structures and access method to be used by the database. It is also known as **physical level**.

(ii) **Conceptual Level** The conceptual level presents a logical view of the entire database and thus, it is also known as **logical level**.

It describes the type data is stored in the database, the relationships among the data and complete view of user's requirements without any concern for physical implementation.

It allows the user to bring all the data in the database together and see it in consistant manner. It hides the complexity of physical storage structures. Database administrator, who must decide what information to keep in the database, uses the logical level of abstraction.

(iii) **External Level** It is the highest level of database abstraction and also known as **view level**. The external level describes a part of database for a particular group of users. In general, most of the users do not require the entire data stored in database, instead, they need to access only a part of the database.

The view level of abstraction exists to simplify their interaction with the system. It provides a powerful and flexible security mechanism by hiding parts of database from certain users.

The user is not aware of the existance of other information that is missing from the view. It permits users to access data in a way that is customized to their needs, so that the same data can be seen by different users in different ways, at the same time.

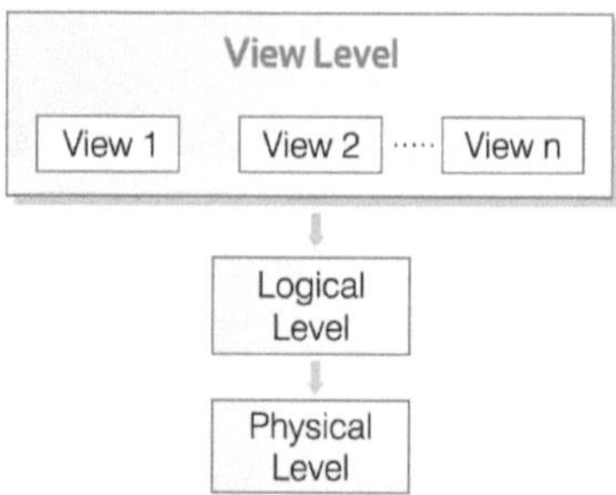

Three Levels of Data Abstraction

To understand the concept of data abstraction, consider the example of the database of a banking organization.

- On the internal level, we find all of the files that store data used by the banking organization, *i.e.*, data of clients, employees of the bank, clients' accounts, pay slips, etc. On this level, we also find the information about the location of data (*For example*, disk location, block, index, etc.)

- On the conceptual level, we find all the data description used, *for example*, the concept of client will be defined by a list of the types of information characterising each client– a code, a last name, a first name, an address, etc., and the content (*For example*, the client accounts.)

- On the external level, we find selections from or categorizations of the database needed by the different users, *for example*, the personnel who prepare the pay slips only have to access to the parts of the database concerning the employees of the bank. They cannot access client accounts.

Data Models

Data model can be defined as an integrated collection of concepts for describing and manipulating data, relationship between data and constraints on the data in an organisation.

A data model provides a way to describe the design of a database at the internal, conceptual and external level.

A data model comprises of three components, which are given below

- A **structural part,** consisting of a set of rules according to which databases can be constructed.

- A **manipulative part,** defining the types of operations that are allowed on the data (this includes the operations that are used for updating or retrieving data from the database and for changing the structure of the database).

- Possibly a set of **integrity rules**, which ensures that the data is accurate.

The purpose of a data model is to represent data and to make the data understandable. The different data models that are used for database management system are:

Hierarchical Data Model

In hierarchical data model, data is organised in a tree-like structure. There is a hierarchy of parent and child data segments. It comprises a set of records connected to one another through links. The link is an association between two or more records. To create links between these records, the hierarchical model uses parent child relationship.

In a hierarchical database, the parent child relationship is One to Many. This restricts a child segment to having only one parent segment but a parent segment can have one or more child segments. Top of the structure consists of a single segment and known as **root segment**. The operations that can be performed on hierarchical model are retrieval, insertion, deletion and modification of records.

Network Data Model

In network data model, data is represented by collection of records and relationships among data are represented by links like hierarchical data model.

The only difference is that in the network model, records are organized as arbitrary graphs rather than trees. In this model, the parent child relationship is Many to Many, i.e. one child segment can have multiple parent segments.

Relational Data Model

In a relational data model, data is stored in different tables with relationship to each other. These tables are called **relations**. These tables communicate and show information which facilitates data search ability, organisation and reporting.

Relational Database

A tabular database in which data is defined so that it can be reorganized and accessed in a number of different ways.

In a relational database, data is stored in different tables with relationships to each other. These tables communicate and share information, which facilitates data search ability, organization and reporting.

Various terms related to relational database are as follows

(i) **Relation** A relation is a table with columns and rows which represent the data items and relationships among them. Relations have three important properties a name, cardinality and a degree.

These properties help us to further define and describe relations

- **Name** The first property of a relation is its name, which is represented by the title or the entity identifier.
- **Cardinality** The second property of a relation is its cardinality, which refers to the number of tuples (rows) in a relation.
- **Degree** The third property of a relation is its degree, which refers to the number of attributes (columns) in each tuple.

(ii) **Domain** A domain is a collection of all possible values from which the values for a given column or an attribute is drawn. A domain is said to be atomic if elements are considered to be indivisible units.

Relational Database Management System (RDBMS)

A Relational Database Management System (RDBMS) is a database management system. It is developed by Dr. E.F. Codd, of IBM's San Jose Research Laboratory.

RDBMS stores data in the form of related tables. RDBMS are powerful because they require few assumptions about how data is related or how it will be extracted from the database.

An important feature of relational database is that a single database can be spread across several tables. Today, popular commercial for large databases include Oracle, Microsoft SQL server, Sybase, MySQL.

(iii) **Attributes** The heading columns of a table are known as attributes. Each attribute of a table has a distinct name.

(iv) **Tuples** The rows in a relation are also known as tuples. Each row or tuple has a set of permitted values for each attribute.

Attributes	Emp_Id	Emp_Name	Emp_Salary	Years
	100	Jim	20000	2
Tuples	101	James	21000	1
	102	Anne	21001	3

Differences between DBMS and RDBMS

DBMS	RDBMS
In DBMS, relationship between two tables or files are maintained programmatically.	In RDBMS, relationship between two tables or files can be specified at the time of table creation.
DBMS does not support client-server architecture.	Most of the RDBMS support client-server architecture.
DBMS does not support distributed databases.	Most of the RDBMS support distributed databases.
In DBMS, there is no security of data.	In RDBMS, there are multiple levels of security such as command level, object level.
Each table is given an extension in DBMS.	Many tables are grouped in one database in RDBMS.

Keys

The key is defined as the column or attribute or a combination of attributes that is used to identify records of the database table. Sometimes we might have to retrieve data from more than one table, in those cases we require to join tables with the help of keys.

A key is also used to arrange the records either in ascending or descending order. It also controls and maintains the integrity of information store in the database.

There are various types of keys, which are as follows

Primary Key

The primary key of a relational table uniquely identifies each record in the table. In some tables, combination of more than one attributes is declared as primary key. In that case, primary key is known as composite key.

Every relation does have a primary key.

For example, in the given table StudentId works as a primary key because it contains Id's, which are unique for each student.

Candidate Key

The set of all attributes which can uniquely identify each tuple of a relation are known as candidate keys. Each table may have one or more candidate keys and one of them will become the primary key. *For example,* column StudentId and the combination of FirstName and LastName work as the candidate keys for the given table.

A candidate key must possess the following properties

  (i) For each row the value of the key must uniquely identify that row.
  (ii) No attribute in the key can be discarded without destroying the property of unique identification.

Alternate Key

From the set of candidate keys after selecting one of the key as primary key, all other remaining keys are known as alternate keys. These keys are also unique but they allow nulls. *For example,* from the candidate keys (StudentId, FirstName and LastName), StudentId chosen as a primary key then the FirstName and LastName column work as a alternate keys.

Foreign Key

A foreign key is a non-key attribute whose value is derived from the primary key of another table. The relationship between two tables is established with the help of foreign key. A table may have multiple foreign keys, and each foreign key can have different referenced table. Foreign keys play an essential role in database design, when tables are broken apart then foreign keys make it possible for them to be reconstructed.

For example, CourseId column of Student table work as a foreign key for student table, as well as a primary key for Course table (referenced table).

Referential Integrity

It concerns the concept of a foreign key. The referential integrity rules states that any foreign key value can only be in one of two states. The usual state of affairs is that the foreign key value refers to a primary key value of some table in the database.

Occasionally and this well depend on the rules of the data owner, a foreign key value can be null.

In this case, we are explicitly saying that either there is no relationship between the objects represented in the database or that this relationship is unknown.

StudentId	FirstName	LastName	CourseId
L0002345	Jim	Black	C002
L0001254	James	Harradine	A004
L0002349	Amanda	Holiand	C002
L0001198	Simon	McCloud	S042
L0023487	Peter	Murray	P301
L0018453	Anne	Norris	S042

Student table

CourseId	CourseName
A004	Accounts
C002	Computing
P301	History
S042	Short Course

Course table

Chapter Practice

Objective Questions

• Multiple Choice Questions

1. DBMS stands for
   (a) Database Microsoft System
   (b) Database Migration System
   (c) Database Management System
   (d) None of the above

Ans. (c) DBMS is the short form of Database Management System. It refers to a category of softwares that store and manage bulk volumes of data.

2. A table can have .... primary key(s).
   (a) 1   (b) 2
   (c) 3   (d) multiple

Ans. (a) A table can have only a single primary key to identify the records.

3. Which of the following is not a DBMS?
   (a) MS-Word
   (b) MySQL
   (c) Oracle
   (d) Microsoft SQL Server

Ans. (a) MySQL , Oracle and Microsoft SQL Server are all DBMS but MS-Word is a documentation software.

4. The total number of columns in a table is called
   (a) cardinality   (b) degree
   (c) spreadsheet   (d) relation

Ans. (b) The term degree refers to the total number of columns in a table.

5. Tables can be linked by
   (a) primary key   (b) candidate key
   (c) alternate key   (d) foreign key

Ans. (d) A foreign key is a common field found in two tables and it links the two tables.

6. The total number of rows in a table is called
   (a) domain   (b) tuple
   (c) field   (d) cardinality

Ans. (d) The total number of rows in a table is called cardinality.

7. If we delete an attribute of a table
   (a) degree increases
   (b) cardinality increases
   (c) degree and cardinality increase
   (d) degree decreases

Ans. (d) Degree is the total number of attributes/columns in a table , so if a column is deleted the degree decreases.

8. Raj wants to make EmpNo and PFNo columns of his table as the primary key. Is it possible?
   (a) Yes
   (b) No
   (c) Yes , possible as a comination of columns
   (d) None of the above

Ans. (c) Two columns cannot be primary key. But a combination of the columns can be primary key.

9. Software that is used to create , manipulate , maintain a relational database management system is called   **(NCERT)**
   (a) documentation software
   (b) spreadsheet software
   (c) RDBMS
   (d) designing software

Ans. (c) A Relational Database Management System (RDBMS) is a software that can be used to maintain , manipulate and create large volumes of data in relations/tables and relationships between them.

10. In a relational data model, a data structure that organises the information about a single topic into rows and columns is
   (a) block   (b) record   (c) tuple   (d) table

Ans. (d) The tables stores the individual domains of data of a database system and thus stores the data and organises it.

11. Which of the following is the drawback of DBMS?
   (a) Improvement in data
   (b) Backup and recovery
   (c) Complexity
   (d) Maintenance of data integrity

Ans. (c) The complex structure of tables , the relationships between them , other database objects and their management is what makes database systems complex and specialised software and people to manage. Database systems are complex, difficult and time-consuming to design.

12. Which of the following component of database system consists of various secondary storage devices on which data is stored?
(a) Hardware (b) User (c) Data (d) Software

Ans. (a) The permanent or secondary storage device is the hard disk or any kind of disk storage that resides in the hardware unit.

13. In files, there is a key associated with each record which is used to differentiate among different records. For every file, there is atleast one set of keys that is unique. Such a key is called
(a) unique key   (b) prime attribute
(c) index key   (d) primary key

Ans. (d) A primary key carries unique values and hence is used to identify the records uniquely.

• Case Based MCQs

Direction *Read the case and answer the following questions.*

14. Anita has created a table "Players" to store the details of players who play in her sports academy . She has planned to create the following table with columns :
PlayerId, PlayerName , Game, Type , AadharNo

Table : Players

PlayerId	PlayerName	Game	Type	AadharNo
P01	Becker	Tennis	Indoor	333444657
P02	Robin	Tennis	Indoor	192900877
P03	Sunetra	Football	Outdoor	214567432
P04	Rakhi	Cricket	Outdoor	111231896

Answer the following questions, which based on the given information.

(i) Which column can she make the primary key?
(a) PlayerId   (b) PlayerName
(c) Game   (d) Type

(ii) Which column(s) can act as candidate key?
(a) Only PlayerId   (b) Only AadharNo
(c) Both (a) and (b)   (d) Type

(iii) Which column is the foreign key in the table?
(a) PlayerName   (b) Type
(c) Game   (d) None of these

(iv) What is the degree of the table?
(a) 1   (b) 2   (c) 3   (d) 5

(v) What will be the cardinality of the table, if two columns are added to the table?
(a) 7   (b) 6
(c) 4   (d) None of these

Ans. (i) (a) The PlayerId column stores unique and non-blank values , hence it can serve as primary key.

(ii) (c) All the field combinations that can serve as primary key for unique identification of records in a table are called candidate keys. Here PlayerId and AadharNo can serve as primary key.
So, these fields can act as candidate keys.

(iii) (d) The concept of foreign key is relevant only when there are multiple tables.

(iv) (d) Degree of a table is the total number of columns, i.e. 5.

(v) (c) The total number of rows in a table is its cardinality, i.e. 4. Adding columns to table increases its degree not cardinality.

15. Mr. Sharma is a new user of database systems . He has created a table storing the details of staff in his office. He is confused about some of the terms related to tables and databases. Help him solving his confusions.

Table : Staff

StaffId	StaffName	Dept	Salary	PF AcNo
1	Mrs. Fernandes	Accts	19500	UP/1108
2	Mr. Das	Sales	45000	WB/6777
3	Ms. Sunita	IT	65000	CH/0097
4	Mr. Roy	Accts	25000	WB/4567

(i) The vertical set storing the departments under the heading "Dept" is called
(a) field   (b) attribute
(c) column   (d) All of these

(ii) What is the cardinality of the table?
(a) 2   (b) 3   (c) 4   (d) 1

(iii) Can "StaffName" column serve as primary key?
(a) No
(b) Yes, only if it stores non-blank and distinct names
(c) Yes, only if it stores only distinct names
(d) Yes

(iv) A tuple carries
(a) a single value
(b) double values
(c) a row of multiple values as a record
(d) None of the above

(v) An attribute which can uniquely identify tuples of the table but is not defined as primary key of the table is called   (NCERT)
(a) primary key   (b) alternate key
(c) forign key   (d) None of these

Ans. (i) (d) The vertical columns of table are also called fields or attributes.

(ii) (c) Cardinality means the number of rows in a table, i.e. 4.

(iii) (b) The primary key of a table has to be unique and NOT NULL .

(iv) (c) A tuple is a horizontal row or record storing all the details of an entity.

(v) (*b*) All the candidate key fields that are not primary key are alternate keys. In a table there can be multiple such fields who can serve as primary key. Such fields are called candidate keys. Among these any one serves as primary key. The rest of the candidate keys are called alternate keys.

PART 2
Subjective Questions

• Short Answer Type Questions

1. What do you understand by the term database?

Ans. A database is a huge collection of data accumulating in a particular system. It comprises of historical data, operational and transactional data. The database grows everyday with the transactions dealing with it.

A database has the following properties
 (i) It is a collection of data elements representing real-world information.
 (ii) It is logical, coherent and internally consistent.

2. What is a DBMS? Expand and explain in short.

Ans. A Database Management System is a software system that enables users to define, create and maintain the database and provides controlled access to this database.

The primary goal of a DBMS is to provide a way to store and retrieve database information that is both convenient and efficient. Data in a database can be added, deleted, changed, sorted or searched, all using a DBMS.

3. What is a table? Also, write the other name of table.

Ans. Table is also called a relation, it is a diagrammatically a matrix of rows and columns that store the data of a particular system. A table is just like a sheet in Excel, that stores data in some columns and rows. The data is arranged under some fields, where each field stores similar kind of data.

4. What do you mean by fields of a table? Give examples.

Ans. A field of a table is simply a vertical column of the table. A field is also called an attribute. It stores similar kind of data. e.g. Name, Class, Marks etc., can be fields of student table, EmpId, Empname, Dept can be fields of Employee table. Each field derives its values from a pool of data which is called as the domain. All the values in a single field will be of same data type.

5. What are records? Also, write the other name of record.

Ans. A record is a horizontal row of a table storing complete data of one entity. It is also called a tuple.
e.g.

2	Mr. Das	Sales	45000

The above record of Mr. Das carries all the information about him. Similarly other records of the table carry data about other employees.
All the records together make up the data of the table.

6. What do you understand by the term degree of a table? Can it change?

Ans. The term degree refers to the total number of columns in a table. Yes the degree changes with addition or deletion of columns.
e.g. If a table "Product" stores the data in columns "PNo, PName, Qty, Price", there are 4 columns , hence the degree will be 4.

7. What do you understand by the term cardinality of a table? How can it be modified?

Ans. The total number of rows of a table is called the cardinality. It gets modified by the addition or deletion of rows. If rows are added to the table the cardinality increases . If rows are deleted the cardinality decreases.

8. What is a primary key? How many primary keys can be there in a table?

Ans. It is a combination of one or more fields in a table that can uniquely identify a record. There can be only one primary key in a table. It plays an important role in identifying the records, because it is the primary key who carries unique values. The criteria for a field to become primary key is : It must be carrying unique and NOT NULL values.

9. What is candidate key?

Ans. All the field combinations that can serve as primary key for unique identification of records in a table are called candidate keys.
For example, If a student table carries "RollNo., Name, Class, AadharNo., AdmissionNo" columns, then columns RollNo., AadharNo. and AdmissionNo can become the candidate keys since all carry unique values.

10. Can we have multiple candidate keys in a table? Give example.

Ans. Yes, we can have multiple candidate primary keys.
e.g. In an Employee table, ENo and AadharNo both can serve as primary key, hence both are candidate keys. Only primary key in a table will be a single field , candidate keys can be multiple.

11. Which fields are regarded as alternate keys?

Ans. All the candidate key fields that are not primary key are alternate keys.
e.g. If a table Employee carries columns "ENo, EName, PFNo, VoterId", then "ENo" is set as primary key and the other candidate keys "PFNo" and "VoterId" will be the alternate keys.

12. Why foreign keys are allowed to have NULL values?   **(NCERT)**

Ans. A foreign key is a field that links two tables . A table may have links to multiple tables . Each link is supported by a value that is common in the two tables . If there is a missing foreign key value for a record , it means the link is missing and no matching values are present. This is perfectly a valid situation, not an error .

13. How many foreign keys can be there in a table?

Ans. A table can have multiple foreign keys depending on the number of tables to which the mother table has links.

Multiple tables can be linked by the foreign key which will be common in all of them . It is by the foreign key that the corresponding values will be obtained from the tables.

14. Write names of few softwares used as DBMS.

Ans. MySQL, Oracle , DB/2, Ingres softwares obey certain common rules of relational algebra. Like they all support most of the codd's rules and support SQL . Some of these softwares like MySQL are free and some like Oracle is proprietary, that it has to be bought.

15. What do you understand by the term domain?

Ans. Domain refers to the pool or set of values from which a field of a table derives its values. e.g. The RollNo field derives its values from the set of integers from 1-100 (approx.). The "Dept" field derives its values from the domain of possible departments and the "Marks" field derives its values from the range of marks in an examination.

16. Give suitable example of a table with sample data and illustrate primary and candidate keys in it.

Ans. **Candidate Key** It is a set of all attributes that uniquely identifies records in a table. Each table may have one or more candidate keys.

Table : Student

AdmNo	RollNo	Name	Class	Marks
2715	1	Rame	12	90
2816	2	Shyeam	11	95
2404	3	Ajay	10	92
2917	4	Tarun	12	94

e.g. In Student table, AdmNo and RollNo both can identify records uniquely. So, both are candidate key.

Primary Key It is a set of one or more attributes that can uniquely identify each tuple of a relation. A relation can have only one primary key.

e.g. In Student table, AdmNo of all students are different. So, we have created AdmNo as primary key.

17. List some commonly used DBMS software packages.

Ans. Some commonly used DBMS software packages are

   (i) MySQL   (ii) Oracle
  (iii) Postgre   (iv) DB2
   (v) MS-SQL   (vi) Sybase

18. Differentiate between an attribute and a tuple with an example.

Ans. The columns of a table are referred to as attributes. It is also known as field which is reserved for a specific piece of data. The rows of a table are referred to as tuples.

	Attributes	
S.No.	Name	Class
1	Raj	10
2	Ajay	12
3	Rahul	11

Tuples ↙

19. What is the difference between degree and cardinality of a table? What is the degree and cardinality of the following table?

Eno	Name	Salary
101	John Fedrick	45000
103	Raya Mazumdar	50600

Ans. **Degree** The number of attributes or columns in a table is called the degree of the table.

The degree of the given table is 3.

Cardinality The number of rows or records in a table is called the cardinality of the table. The cardinality of the given table is 2.

20. Mention atleast three limitations of DBMS.

Ans. Some limitations of DBMS are given below

   (i) **High Cost** DBMS requires various software, hardware and highly intelligent people for operating and maintaining the database system. It increases its cost.

  (ii) **Database Failure** If database is corrupted due to power failure or any other reason, our valuable data may be lost or whole system stops.

 (iii) **Data Quality** With increased number of users accessing data directly. There are enormous opportunities for users to damage data. So, it is not easy to provide a strategy to support multiple users to update data simultaneously.

• Long Answer Type Questions

21. Explain the role of database management system in maintaining huge volumes of data of different domains. Explain your views using an example.

Ans. A database management system is a specialised software that helps maintain large volumes of data pertaining to a real life system . Examples of such systems include business houses , transport systems, libraries , schools etc.

It not only stores bulk data in structured way but also helps to add , modify ,search , update and delete data from such databases. Examples of DBMS softwares are MySQL , Microsoft SQL Server , Oracle etc.

Application program accesses the data stored in the database by sending request to the DBMS.

For example, MySQL, INGRES, MS-ACCESS etc.

The purpose of a Database Management System is to bridge the gap between information and data. The data stored in memory or on disk must be converted to usable information.

22. A table "Sports" exists with 3 columns and 5 rows. What is its degree and cardinality? 2 rows are added to the table and 1 column deleted. What will be the degree and cardinality now?

Ans. The term degree refers to the total number of columns in a table. The term cardinality refers to the total number of rows in a table.

Initially, Sports table has 3 columns and 5 rows, so

Degree : 3

Cardinality : 5

After operations, 2 rows are added to the table and 1 column deleted.

Now, degree : 2 cardinality : 7.

23. Differentiate the terms primary key and candidate key.

Ans. Differences between primary key and candidate key are

Primary key	Candidate key
A primary key is a single field in a table that is used to identify the records uniquely.	A candidate key is a set of columns who are eligible for unique identification of records.
Only one field among the candidate keys is selected as primary key.	A table can have multiple candidate keys.
Primary key of a table is used in linking the data of the table to another table.	Candidate keys do not have such role.

24. Explain by an example how foreign key is useful for bringing data from multiple tables?

Ans. Consider the two tables given below

Table : Student

RollNo	Name	Class	Marks	AddressID
1	Rohan	12ScA	78.5	A1
2	Smita	11ComC	67.7	A2
3	Priya	12HumA	82.6	A3

Table : Address

AddressID	Place	State	Contact
A1	Pahargunj	Delhi	9876745655
A2	Kolkata	WB	9434566778
A3	Barnala	Punjab	9433534038

Referring to the above tables , if we look for Place to which "Priya" belongs" , we can link the tables by the foreign key "AddressID" of the Student table to get place as "Barnala" by the AddressID "A3". So, a foreign key helps in bringing data from multiple tables.

Chapter Test

Multiple Choice Questions

1. The other name for a table is
  (a) database   (b) relation
  (c) domain   (d) degree

2. A DBMS is used for
  (a) designing   (b) image merging
  (c) compression of file   (d) None of these

3. Special value that is stored when actual data value is unknown for an attribute. **(NCERT)**
  (a) None   (b) NULL
  (c) NaN   (d) None of these

4. The foreign key of a table
  (a) has unique values
  (b) has integer type values
  (c) has a linking column in another table
  (d) None of the above

5. The number of rows of a table is
  (a) limited
  (b) not limited
  (c) can be restricted while table creation
  (d) None of the above

Short Answer Type Questions

6. What is the use of foreign key field?

7. What are the components of a database system?

8. Can a primary key be alternate key?

9. While creating a table Rahul has restricted duplicate values in one of the columns. Can he make the column as primary key? Justify your answer.

10. Explain the term relation.

Long Answer Type Questions

11. Considering the following tables

Table : STUDENT

RollNo	Name	Class	Section	Registration_ID
11	Mohan	XI	1	IP-101-15
12	Sohan	XI	2	IP-104-15
21	John	XII	1	CS-103-14
22	Meena	XII	2	CS-101-14
23	Juhi	XII	2	CS-101-10

Table : PROJECT

ProjectNo	PName	Submission_Date
101	Airline Database	12/01/2018
102	Library Database	12/01/2018
103	Employee Database	15/01/2018
104	Student Database	12/01/2018
105	Inventory Database	15/01/2018
106	Railway Database	15/01/2018

Table : PROJECT ASSIGNED

Registration_ID	ProjectNo
IP-101-15	101
IP-104-15	103
CS-103-14	102
CS-101-14	105
CS-101-10	104

Answer the questions, which based on above information.

(i) Name primary key of each table.

(ii) Find foreign key(s) in table PROJECT ASSIGNED.

(iii) Is there any alternate key in table STUDENT? Give justification for your answer.

(iv) Can a user assign duplicate value to the field RollNo of STUDENT table? Jusify.

12. An organisation wants to create a database EMP_DEPENDENT to maintain following details about its employees and their dependent.

EMPLOYEE(AadharNumber, Name, Address, Department,EmployeeID)

DEPENDENT(EmployeeID, DependentName, Relationship)

(i) Name the attributes of EMPLOYEE, which can be used as candidate keys.

(ii) The company wants to retrieve details of dependent of a particular employee. Name the tables and the key which are required to retrieve this detail.

(iii) What is the degree of EMPLOYEE and DEPENDENT relation?

13. What are the major components of a database system?

14. Differentiate the terms DBMS and RDBMS.

15. In a multiplex, movies are screened in different auditoriums. One movie can be shown in more than one auditorium. In order to maintain the record of movies, the multiplex maintains a relational database consisting of two relations *viz.* CINEMA and PEOPLE respectively as shown below:

CINEMA(Movie_ID, MovieName, ReleaseDate)

PEOPLE(AudiNo, Movie_ID, Seats, ScreenType, TicketPrice)

(i) Is it correct to assign Movie_ID as the primary key in the CINEMA relation? If no, then suggest an appropriate primary key.

(ii) Is it correct to assign AudiNo as the primary key in the PEOPLE relation? If no, then suggest appropriate primary key.

(iii) Is there any foreign key in any of these relations?

Answers

Multiple Choice Questions

1. (b)   2. (d)   3. (b)   4. (c)   5. (b)

For Detailed Solutions

Scan the code

CHAPTER 02

Introduction to MySQL and SQL

In this Chapter...

- MySQL
- Structured Query Language (SQL)
- SQL Commands
- Data Types

MySQL

Most organizations track different types of information, like; information about their employees, clients, projects and any other terms, which support or which might support their programs and services. Managing this information is crucial.

A DBMS (Database Management System) allows the user to manage and use a vast variety of information easily.
DBMS also provides a centralized control of its operational data.

DBMS is easy to set-up, easy to manipulate and easy to use. There are many DBMSs available in the market such as MySQL, INGRES, POSTGRES, DB2, Oracle, etc, among them MySQL is very popular database management system.

MySQL is an open source Relational Database Management System(RDBMS) based on SQL(Structured Query Language).

In MySQL database, information is stored in tables and runs virtually on all platforms including Linux, Unix and Windows.

MySQL provides many features such as storing, maintaining and controlling data in a secured environment. It is a fast, reliable, scalable substitute to many of the commercial RDBMSs available today. MySQL works with many languages like PHP, Perl, C, C++, Java etc.

History of MySQL

MySQL was introduced by a software company MySQL AB, founded by **David Axmark**, **Allan Larsson** and **Michael Widenius** in the year 1994 in Sweden. Sun Microsystems (a well known ZJava development company) acquired MySQL

AB on 26-February-2008. MySQL was first released on 23-May-1995, for personal usage based on ISAM (Indexed Sequential Access Method).

It supports the basic principles of database and data manipulation used to retrieve, insert and update stored data. Being an open source anyone can use and change the software for their needs.

It supports the basic principles of database and data manipulation using SQL statements.

MySQL 8.0.16 was the latest version of MySQL and it is available free of cost on Internet.

Some of the MySQL versions are as follows

Versions	Released Date
MySQL 3.20.0	May 1997
MySQL 3.23.0	August 1999
MySQL 3.23.32	January 2001
MySQL 4.1	October 2004
MySQL 5.0	October 2005
MySQL 5.1	November 2008
MySQL 5.5	December 2010
MySQL 5.6	February 2013
MySQL 8.0.16	April 2018

Components of MySQL

A database is a structured collection of data, the vast amount of information. To add, access, and process data stored in a computer database, you need a database management system such as MySQL server.

Information system is the key role of database management system and database server is the key to solve the problems of information management.

MySQL can be used for variety of applications but it is mostly used for the web applications on the Internet.

MySQL database system consists of the following three components

Server (MySQL server)

MySQL server is an engine which provides access to databases, responsible for creating, managing database, executing and returning queries and maintaining security together with additional tools to manage multiple MySQL servers.

Clients

A client is a program that connects to the database server and issue queries in a pre-specified format. In MySQL, you can enter command-line queries to manage user permissions and utilities to import and export MySQL database.

Client Library

A client library is an Application Programming Interface (API) where a client can write their own programs using a programming language like C, C++, Java, etc.

Working of MySQL

MySQL database works on client/server architecture. It is installed on a server (i.e. single machine), but it can provide the database facility to a variety of clients at different locations.

MySQL server can be accessed directly *via* various client interfaces, which send SQL statements to the server and then display the results to the user.

The following figure shows the working of MySQL server

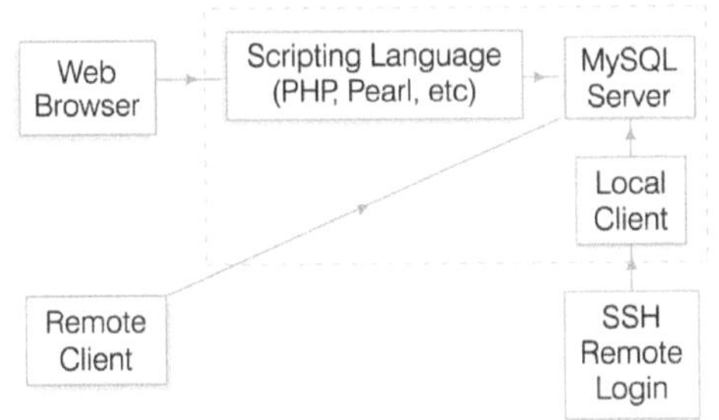

(i) **Local Client** It is a program on the same machine as the server. *For example*, Command Line MySQL client software.

(ii) **Scripting Language** It can pass SQL queries to the server and display the result.

For example, PHP, Perl, Python, etc.

(iii) **Remote Client** It is a program on different machine that can be connected to the server and display the result.

(iv) **Remote Login** It allows connecting to the server machine to run one of its local clients.

(v) **Web Browser** We can use a web browser and scipts that someone has written.

Features of MySQL

MySQL is one of the top most database available in the market today. It is a relational database with many advanced features and options.

Some of the key features of MySQL are given below

Speed

MySQL is a very fast and reliable database program that supports clump servers for several demanding application programs.

The speed of MySQL has been backed up by a large number of benchmark tests.

Open Source

It is an open source database system which means anyone can use it without any cost.

One of the most benefit of MySQL includes its wide availability in the market with no ownership cost. MySQL is quite customizable due to the fact that developers can alter its code in order to satisfy their needs.

Ease to Use

MySQL is a high performance but relatively simple database system and is less complex to setup or examine than larger database systems.

Query Language Support

ANSI (American National Standard Institute) standard SQL is an easy language to use because of its straight forward and simple syntax. MySQL supports standard based SQL (Structured Query Language) for querying and managing relational databases.

Security

MySQL is secured as all its access passwords are stored in an encrypted format restricting any unauthorized access to the system.

It also encrypts the transactions so eavesdroppers and data maintenance tools cannot replicate or regenerate the database transactions once they are processed.

Cross Platform Portability

MySQL is easily installable and operable on different platforms including Linux, Windows, OS2, Solaris etc. It also contains APIs for integration with various programming languages like C, C++, PHP, Java, Perl, Python and Ruby etc.

Licensing

MySQL works under the GPL (General Public License) i.e., the users can enjoy the opportunity at free of cost.

Connectivity

MySQL is a relational client/server database system. There is a database server (MySQL) and arbitrarily many clients (application programs), which communicate with the server using several protocols i.e., they query data, save changes etc.

Structured Query Language (SQL)

SQL is used by all programs and users to access data within the MySQL database. There is a structure to this language, it uses english phrases to define an action, but uses math-like symbols to make comparisons.

For example,

```
SELECT * FROM Table;
```

SQL was initially developed at IBM by **Donald D. Chamberlin** and **Raymond F. Boyce** in the early 1970s.

This version initially called SEQUEL (Structured English Query Language), was designed to manipulate and retrieve data stored in IBM's original RDBMS.

In the late 1970s, Oracle Corporation saw the potential of the concepts described by codd, Chamberlin and Boyce and developed their own SQL-based RDBMS with aspirations of selling it to the various U.S. government agencies.

In June 1979, Oracle Corporation introduced the first commercially available implementation of SQL, Oracle V2 for VAX computers. The American National Standards Institute (ANSI) adopted SQL as the standard language for RDBMSs in 1986.

The International Standards Organization (ISO) has also adopted SQL as the standard language for RDBMSs.

Characteristics of SQL

Main characteristics of SQL are given below

- SQL is an ANSI and ISO standard computer language for creating and manipulating databases.
- SQL allows the user to create, update, delete and retrieve data from a database.
- SQL is very simple and easy to learn.
- SQL is used specifically for relational databases.
- SQL works with database programs like DB2, Oracle, MS-Access, Sybase Microsoft SQL Server, etc.

SQL Commands

In order to access data from MySQL database, all applications, programmers and users must use Structured Query Language (SQL). SQL commands are the instructions used to communicate with the database to perform specific task that work with data. SQL commands can be used not only for searching the database but also to perform various other functions like, create tables, add data to tables, modify data, drop the table, set permissions for users and many more.

SQL commands can be classified into following categories

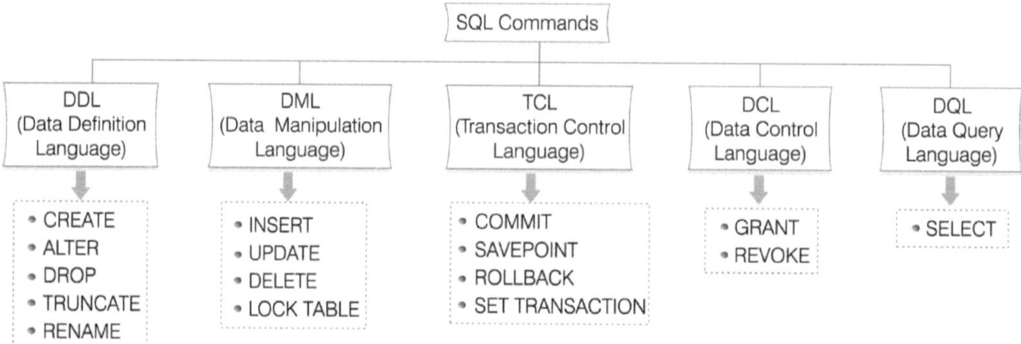

Data Definition Language (DDL)

DDL is used to define the structure of your tables and other objects in the database. In DBMS, it is used to specify a database schema as a set of definitions (expressed in DDL), In SQL, DDL allows you to create, alter and destroy database objects.

Basically, a data definition language is a computer language used to create and modify the structure of database objects in a database. These database objects include views, schemas, tables, indexes, etc.

This term is also known as **data description language** in some contexts, as it describes the fields and records in a database table.

Data definition language consists of various commands that lets you to perform some specified tasks as follows

- (i) **CREATE** Used to create objects in the database.
- (ii) **ALTER** Used to alter the structure of the database table. This command can add up additional column, drop existing columns and even change the data type of columns involved in a database table.
- (iii) **DROP** Used to delete objects from the database.
- (iv) **TRUNCATE** Used to remove all records from a table.
- (v) **RENAME** Used to rename an object.

Data Manipulation Language (DML)

DML provides various commands used to access and manipulate data in existing database. This manipulation involves inserting data into database tables, retrieving existing data, deleting data from existing tables and modifying existing data. DML is mostly incorporated in SQL database. The basic goal of DML is to provide efficient human interaction with the system.

The DMLs are of two types

Procedural DMLs These require a user to specify what data is needed and how to get it.

Non-Procedural DMLs These require a user to specify what data is needed without specifying how to get it.

Various data manipulation language commands are as follows

- (i) **INSERT** Used to insert data into a table.
- (ii) **UPDATE** Used to update existing data within a table.
- (iii) **DELETE** Used to delete all records from a table, the space of the records remains.
- (iv) **LOCK TABLE** Used to control concurrency.

Differences between DDL and DML

DDL	DML
DDL is the abbreviation of Data Definition Language.	DML is the abbreviation of Data Manipulation Language.
It is used to create and modify the structure of database objects in database.	It is used to retrieve, store, modify, delete, insert and update data in database.
DDL commands allow us to perform tasks related to data definition.	DML commands are used to manipulate data.
For example, CREATE, ALTER, and DROP commands.	*For example*, SELECT, UPDATE, and INSERT commands.

Transaction Control Language (TCL)

TCL is playing an important role in SQL. TCL commands are used to manage transactions in database. These are also used to manage the changes made by DML statements. It allows statements to be grouped together into logical transactions. A transactions is a single unit of work.

Each individual statement is a transaction. If a transaction is successful, all of the data modifications made during the transaction are committed and became a permanent part of the database. If a transaction encounters an error and must be cancelled or rolled back, then all of the data modifications are erased. To manage all these operations, transaction control language commands are used.

Various transaction control statements are as follows

- (i) **COMMIT** Used to save the work done.
- (ii) **SAVEPOINT** Used to identify a point in a transaction to which you can later rollback.
- (iii) **ROLLBACK** Used to restore database to original since the last COMMIT.
- (iv) **SET TRANSACTION** It establishes properties for the current transactions.

Data Control Language (DCL)

DCL commands are used to assign security levels in database which involves multiple user setups.

They are used to grant defined role and access privilages to the users.

There are two kinds of user in the schema

Users They work with the data, but cannot change the structure of the schema. They write data manipulation language.

Admin They can change the structure of the schema and control access to the schema objects. They write data definition language.

Basically, the DCL command of the SQL language is used to create privileges to allow users access to and manipulation of the database. Two types of DCL commands are

- (i) **GRANT** Used to give user's access privileges to database.
- (ii) **REVOKE** Used to withdraw access privileges given with the GRANT command.

Data Query Language (DQL)

DQL is used to fetch the data from the database. It uses only one command **SELECT**. This command helps you to select the attribute based on the condition described by the WHERE clause.

Creating a Database

Creating a database is an easier task. You need to just type the name of the database in a **CREATE DATABASE** command.

Syntax

```
CREATE DATABASE [IF NOT EXISTS]<database
_name>;
```

CREATE DATABASE command will create an empty database with the specified name and would not contain any table.

IF NOT EXISTS is an optional part of this statement which prevents you from an error if there exists a database with the given name in the database catalog.

For example, `mysql>CREATE DATABASE BOOK;`

Output Query OK, 1 row affected <0.01 sec>

Select a Database

Creating a database is not enough for use. Before working with tables, first you have to select the database. The only thing need to be considered before selecting a database is that it must already exist. To select a database **USE** command is used.

Syntax `USE <database_name>;`

For example, `mysql>USE ENGBOOK;`

where, **USE** command makes the specified database as a current working database and **ENGBOOK** is the database name.

Output Database changed

Creating a Table

Database is a collection of tables. The main purpose for creating tables is to store information in an orderly fashion. Each database table consists of columns and rows-just like a graphical table.

The columns specify what data is going to be stored, while the rows contain the actual data. Tables are created using CREATE TABLE command.

Syntax

```
CREATE TABLE table_name
(
    column_name1 data_type(size),
    column_name2 data_type(size),
        ⋮
);
```

Here,

CREATE TABLE defines a new table.

table_name defines the name of a table.

column_name defines the name of a column.

data_type specify that which type of data can be contained in a particular column.

For example,

```
mysql > CREATE TABLE STUDENT
(
Student_Code INTEGER(5),
```

```
Student_Name CHAR(20),
Sex CHAR(1),
Grade CHAR(2),
Total_Marks DECIMAL
);
```

Output

Query OK, 0 rows affected <0.06 sec>

Displaying the Table Structure

DESCRIBE or **DESC** command is used to verify the structure of a table that you have created.

This command display the column names, available data items with their data types.

Syntax

```
DESCRIBE <table_name>;
   or
DESC <table_name>;
```

For example,

```
mysql>DESC STUDENT;
```

Output

```
+--------------+------------+------+-----+---------+-------+
| Field        | Type       | Null | Key | Default | Extra |
+--------------+------------+------+-----+---------+-------+
| Student_Code | INTEGER(5) | NO   | PRI |         |       |
| Student_Name | CHAR(20)   | YES  | MARY|         |       |
| Sex          | CHAR(1)    | YES  |     |         |       |
| Grade        | CHAR(2)    | YES  |     |         |       |
| Total_Marks  | DECIMAL    | YES  |     |         |       |
+--------------+------------+------+-----+---------+-------+
5 rows in set (0.08 sec)
```

Data Types

A data type is a data storage format that can contain a specific type or range of values. The fields within a database often require a specific type of data to be input.

For example, a school's record for a student may use a character data type for the students first and last name.

The student's date of admission and date of birth would be stored in a date format, while his or her marks in each subject may be stored as a numeric.

Some mainly used data types in MySQL are as follows

  (i) Numeric data type

 (ii) String or Text data type

(iii) Date and time data type

Numeric Data Type

It allows the database server to store numbers such as integers and real numbers in a column.

For example, age of the students, numbers obtained in subjects etc.

Types	Length in Bytes	Minimum Value (Signed)	Maximum Value (Signed)	Minimum Value (Unsigned)	Maximum Value (Unsigned)
TINYINT	1	-128	127	0	255
SMALLINT	2	-32768	32767	0	65535
MEDIUMINT	3	-8388608	8388607	0	16777215
INT	4	-2147483648	2147483647	0	4294967295
BIGINT	8	-9223372036854775808	9223372036854775807	0	18446744073709551615

FLOAT (N,D) A small number with floating decimal point. It cannot be unsigned. It's size is 4 bytes. Here, N represents the total number of digits (including decimals) and D represents the number of decimals.

DOUBLE (N,D) A large number with floating decimal point. It cannot be unsigned. It's size is 8 bytes. Here, N represents the total number of digits and D represents the number of decimals.

DECIMAL (N,D) An unpacked floating point number that cannot be unsigned. In decimal, each decimal number corresponds to one byte. Here, N is the total number of digits and D is the number of decimals.

String/Text Data Type

It allows the database server to store string values such as Name of the students, Address etc.

Types	Description	Display Format	Range in characters
CHAR	Contains non-binary strings. Length is fixed as you declare while creating a table. When stored, they are right-padded with spaces to the specified length.	Trailing spaces are removed.	The length can be any value from 0 to 255.
VARCHAR	Contains non-binary strings. Columns are variable length strings.	As stored.	A value from 0 to 255 before MySQL 5.0.3, and 0 to 65,535 in 5.0.3 and later versions.

Date and Time Data Type

It allows the database server to store a date using the fields YEAR, MONTH and DAY in the format YYYY-MM-DD.

For example, Date of admission, Date of birth etc.

Types	Description	Display Format	Range
TIME	Use when you need only time information	HH:MM:SS	−838:59:59 to 838:59:59
DATETIME	Use when you need values containing both date and time information.	YYYY-MM-DD HH:MM:SS	'1000-01-01 00:00:00' to '9999-12-31 23:59:59'
DATE	Use when you need only date information.	YYYY-MM-DD	'1000-01-01' to '9999-12-31'
TIMESTAMP	Values are converted from the current time zone to UTC (Co-ordinated Universal Time), while storing and converted back from UTC to the current time zone when retrieved.	YYYY-MM-DD HH:MM:SS	'1970-01-01 00:00:01' UTC to '2038-01-19 03:14:07' UTC
YEAR	The year type is a 1-byte type used to represent year values. It can be declared as year (2) or year (4) to specify a display width of two or four characters. If no width is given, the default is 4 characters.	4444	1901 to 2155

Chapter Practice

Objective Questions

• Multiple Choice Questions

1. SQL stands for
(a) Standard Queue Language
(b) Standard Query Language
(c) Structured Query Language
(d) None of the above

Ans. (c) SQL stands for Structured Query Language . It is used to perform different operations with databases and the data held in tables. It can perform operations like search, delete , update etc.

2. The command CREATE belongs to
(a) DDL
(b) DML
(c) TCL
(d) DCL

Ans. (a) The CREATE command belongs to DDL category.

3. MySQL is a
(a) open source software
(b) proprietary software
(c) shareware
(d) None of the above

Ans. (a) MySQL is a free and open source software.

4. There are .... categories of SQL commands.
(a) 2
(b) 3
(c) 1
(d) 4

Ans. (d) SQL commands are divided into 4 categories : DDL , DML , TCL and DCL.

5. The command used to remove objects from a database is
(a) DELETE
(b) DROP
(c) REMOVE
(d) CLEAR

Ans. (b) The DROP command used to remove objects completely from a database.

6. In MySQL, commands can be written in
(a) uppercase
(b) lowercase
(c) title case
(d) any case

Ans. (d) In MySQL, commands are not case- sensitive , hence commands can be written in any case.

7. The command to modify data in SQL
(a) ALTER
(b) UPDATE
(c) CREATE
(d) None of these

Ans. (b) The UPDATE command is used in SQL to make changes to the data of a table.

8. Which of the following is not a feature of MySQL?
(a) Cross platform
(b) User friendly
(c) Open source
(d) License fee is to be paid for use

Ans. (d) MySQL does not need any license fee to be paid for use.

9. A .... declares that an index in one table is related to that in another table. **(NCERT)**
(a) foreign key
(b) composite key
(c) secondary key
(d) primary key

Ans. (a) A foreign key is a linking column in two tables that indicates the relation between the two tables.

10. Given the table Student **(NCERT)**

RollNumber	SName	DateofBirth	Guid
1	Atharv Ahuja	2003-05-15	444444444444
3	Taleem Shah	2002-02-28	101010101010
4	John Dsouza	2003-08-18	333333333333
5	Ali Shah	2003-07-05	101010101010
6	Manika Pal	2002-03-10	466444444666

What is the degree of the table?
(a) 2
(b) 1
(c) 3
(d) 4

Ans. (d) Degree is the number of columns in a table . The Student table contains 4 columns, so degree is 4.

• Case Based MCQs

Direction *Read the case and answer the following questions.*

11. Mr. Subramaniyam is new to databases and its formation, using softwares . He is confused between certain terms related to database management softwares and the SQL commands used in them. Help him in understanding the concepts.

(i) Which of the following are not DBMS?
   (a) MySQL   (b) Adobe Reader
   (c) Oracle   (d) DB/2

(ii) RDBMS stands for
   (a) Real Database Making Software
   (b) Reading and Database Making Software
   (c) Relational Database Management System
   (d) Real Database Making Structure

(iii) DML commands help to
   (a) add records
   (b) remove a table
   (c) create a database
   (d) remove a database

(iv) He wanted to know the command to be used to delete the records of a table, the command is
   (a) REMOVE   (b) ADD
   (c) DELETE   (d) DROP

(v) He wanted to create a table Sports where he wanted to have SportsID as the primary key. Can he insert two SportIDs with same value ? **(NCERT)**
   (a) Yes
   (b) No
   (c) Yes, if SportsID is foreign key
   (d) Yes , if SportsID does not store numbers

Ans. (i) (*b*) Adobe reader is a software that helps to create platform independent document files.
   (ii) (*a*) DML or Data Manipulation Language commands help to add, modify , delete and view records of a table.
   (iiii) (*c*) RDBMS stands for Relational Database Management System.
   (iv) (*c*) The command is DELETE that delete records of a table.
   (v) (*b*) Primary keys cannot have duplicate values.

12. Mrs. Rama wants to create two tables Employee and Work storing details of employees and their work locations as follows

Table : Employee

EmpId	EmpName	Dept	LocationID
1	Mrs. Aritri	Accts	L1
2	Mr. Rai	Sales	L2
3	Ms. Sunetra	IT	L3
4	Mr. Jacob	Accts	L2
5	Mr. Subir	IT	L3

Table : Work

LocationID	Location	Type
L1	Switzerland	Abroad
L2	Bangalore	Country
L3	Kolkata	Country

(i) Which column links the two tables?
   (a) LocationID   (b) Type
   (c) EmpName   (d) EmpId

(ii) Which column can be the primary key of the Employee table? **(NCERT)**
   (a) EmpName   (b) Dept
   (c) EmpId   (d) LocationID

(iii) What command she can use to create the tables?
   (a) ALTER   (b) CREATE
   (c) APPEND   (d) None of these

(iv) Which column can be the primary key of the Work table ? **(NCERT)**
   (a) LocationID
   (b) Location
   (c) Type
   (d) Primary key is not required

(v) If she wants to add a column to the table , the command that she would use , will be of which category ?
   (a) DDL   (b) TCL
   (c) DML   (d) DCL

Ans. (i) (*a*) The locationID is the column that common in both the tables and can be used to link both the tables.
   (ii) (*c*) Primary key must be unique and carry not null values. It should be capable of identifying the records uniquely. Hence, EmpId can be the primary key.
   (iii) (*b*) The CREATE is a DDL command that creates a table.
   (iv) (*a*) The LocationID is the column that can uniquely identify the records of the Work table, hence it qualifies for being the primary key.
   (v) (*a*) DDL or Data Definition Language commands are those that help to define database objects and their schema.

PART 2

Subjective Questions

• Short Answer Type Questions

1. Can a foreign key column be removed? What will happen if such a column is removed?

Ans. Yes, a foreign key column can be removed.

When a referenced foreign key is deleted or updated, respectively, the columns of all rows referencing that key will be set to NULL. The column must allow NULL or this update will fail.

You can delete a foreign key constraint in SQL Server by using SQL Server Management Studio or Transact-SQL. Deleting a foreign key constraint removes the requirement to enforce referential integrity.

2. What are the different categories of SQL commands?

Ans. The SQL command categories are
   (i) **DDL** Data Defination Language
   (ii) **DML** Data Manipulation Language
   (iii) **TCL** Transaction Control Language
   (iv) **DCL** Data Control Language

3. Name few other softwares that belong to the same category as MySQL.

Ans. MySQL is a database management software . Other softwares that belong to the same category are Oracle, MS-Access , DB/2 , Microsoft SQL Server, etc.

4. Describe the terms
   (i) Domain   (ii) DB2

Ans. (i) **Domain** It is a set of possible values for an attribute. A domain is said to be atomic if elements of the domain are considered as indivisible units.
   (ii) **DB2** It is a Relational Database Management System (RDBMS), fully-featured, high performance database capable of handling large quantities of data and concurrently serving many users.

5. Write one difference between data and information.

Ans. Data is raw, unorganised facts that need to be processed. Data can be something simple and random. It is useless until it is organised. *For example*, each student's test score is one piece of data. When data is processed, organised, structured or presented in a given context so as to make it useful, it is called information.

6. What are the integer data types in MySQL?

Ans. MySQL supports the following integer data types
   (i) TINYINT
   (ii) SMALLINT
   (iii) MEDIUMINT
   (iv) INT
   (v) BIGINT

7. State and explain the command that opens a database for working.

Ans. The USE command opens a database for working in it. A database must be opened using the USE command before anything can be done on its components. It belongs to DDL category.

8. What the float data type variations available in MySQL?

Ans. The float data type variations are
   (i) **DOUBLE** (N,D) A large number with floating decimal point. It cannot be unsigned. It's size is 8 bytes. Here, N represents the total number of digits and D represents the number of decimals.
   (ii) **DECIMAL** (N,D) An unpacked floating point number that cannot be unsigned. In decimal, each decimal number corresponds to one byte. Here, N is the total number of digits and D is the number of decimals.

9. In a sports academy there are two tables to store data

   Sport(Sport_ID, SportName,Charges)

   Sportsman(SP_ID,Sport_ID,SP_Name,Address)

   (i) Is it correct to assign Sport_ID as the primary key in the Sport relation? If no, then suggest an appropriate primary key.

   (ii) Is it correct to assign SP_ID as the primary key in the Sportsman relation? If no, then suggest appropriate primary key.

Ans. (i) Yes, it is correct to assign Sport_ID as primary key as it will contain unique and not null values and it can be used for identifying the records.
   (ii) Yes, it is correct to assign SP_ID as primary key as it will contain unique and not null values and it can be used for identifying the records.

10. An organisation wants to create a database STAFFDB to maintain following details about its employees and their families.   **(NCERT)**

   Staff(Aadhar, SName, Location , Dept, StaffID)

   Family(StaffID, DependentName, Relation)

   (i) The attributes of STAFF, which can be used as candidate keys.

   (ii) The company wants to retrieve details of dependent of a particular staff. Name the tables and the key which are required to retrieve this detail.

Ans. (i) **Candidate Keys** Aadhar, StaffID
   (ii) **Tables required** Staff , Family
       Key StaffID

11. Distinguish between UPDATE and ALTER commands.

Ans. Differences between UPDATE and ALTER Commands are as follows

UPDATE	ALTER
Belongs to DML category.	Belongs to DDL category.
Modified data of a table.	Modifies structure of the table .
Data can be modified with new data or expressions.	Columns can be added, modified , removed and renamed.

12. Explain the DML commands.

Ans. There are some DML commands are
   (i) **SELECT** Used to retrieve data from a database.
   (ii) **INSERT** Used to insert data into a table.
   (iii) **UPDATE** Used to update existing data within a table.
   (iv) **DELETE** Used to delete all records from a table, the space of the records remains.

13. Write the important characteristics of SQL.

Ans. There are some important characteristics of SQL are

(i) SQL is used specifically for relational databases.

(ii) SQL statements end with a semicolon (;).

(iii) SQL is an ANSI and ISO standard computer language for creating and manipulating databases.

(iv) SQL allows the user to create, update, delete and retrieve data from a database.

(v) SQL is very simple and easy to learn.

14. Differentiate DELETE and DROP commands of SQL.

Ans. Differences between DELETE and DROP cammands are

DELETE	DROP
Belongs to DML category.	Belongs to DDL category.
Used to remove records from a table.	Used to remove database objects like tables and databases.
Works with components of a table.	Works with entire database objects.

15. Differentiate between COMMIT and ROLLBACK command.

Ans. COMMIT command is used to permanent all the changes made by DML commands, while ROLLBACK means that it undoes all changes since the beginning of a transaction or since a save point.

16. What are DDL and DML?

Ans. **DDL (Data Definition Language)** is a part of SQL, which provides commands for creating, altering and dropping the tables. Different DDL commands are CREATE, ALTER, DROP and RENAME.

DML (Data Manipulation Language) is a part of SQL, which provides commands for inserting, deleting and updating the information in a database. Different DML commands are SELECT, UPDATE, INSERT.

• Long Answer Type Questions

17. Explain the major components of a database system.

Ans. The major components of a database system are Hardware, Software, Data, Database Access Language, Procedures and Users all together form the components of a DBMS.

Let us discuss the components one by one clearly.

Hardware The hardware is the actual computer system used for keeping and accessing the database. The conventional DBMS hardware consists of secondary storage devices such as hard disks. Databases run on the range of machines from micro computers to mainframes.

Software Software is the actual DBMS between the physical database and the users of the system. All the requests from the user for accessing the database are handled by DBMS.

Data It is an important component of the database management system. The main task of DBMS is to process the data. Databases are used to store the data, retrieved and updated to and from the databases.

Users There are a number of users who can access or retrieve the data on demand using the application and the interfaces provided by the DBMS.

The users of the database can be classified into different groups

- Native Users
- Online Users
- Sophisticated Users
- Specialized Users
- Application Users
- DBA- Database Administrator

The components of DBMS are given below in pictorial form

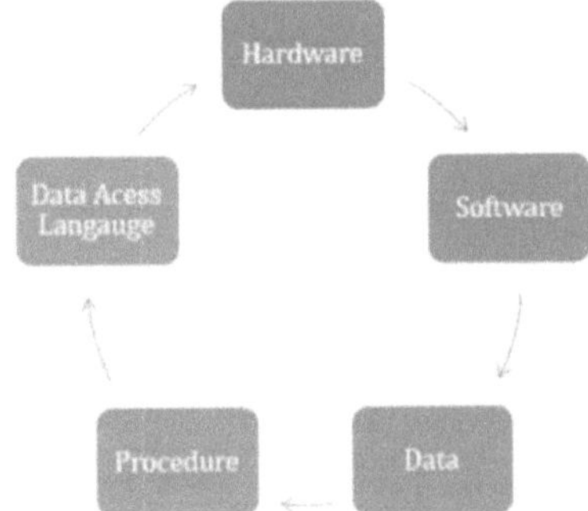

18. Explain the features of MySQL software.

Ans. The features of MySQL are as follows

(i) **Speed** MySQL is a very fast and reliable database program that supports clump servers for several demanding application programs. The speed of MySQL has been backed up by a large number of benchmark tests.

(ii) **Open Source** It is an open source database system which means anyone can use it without any cost. One of the most benefit of MySQL includes its wide availability in the market with no ownership cost. MySQL is quite customisable due to the fact that developers can alter its code in order to satisfy their needs.

(iii) **Ease to Use** MySQL is a high performance but relatively simple database system and is less complex to setup or examine than larger database systems.

(iv) **Query Language Support** ANSI (American National Standard Institute) standard SQL is an easy language to use because of its straight forward and simple syntax. MySQL supports standard based SQL (Structured Query Language) for querying and managing relational databases.

(v) **Security** MySQL is secured as all its access passwords are stored in an encrypted format restricting any unauthorised access to the system. It also encrypts the transactions so eavesdroppers and data maintenance tools cannot replicate or regenerate the database transactions once they are processed.

(vi) **Cross Platform Portability** MySQL is easily installable and operable on different platforms including Linux, Windows, OS2, Solaris etc. It also contains APIs for integration with various programming languages like C, C++, PHP, Java, Perl, Python and Ruby etc.

19. Write the different SQL commands with their uses

Ans. There are different types of SQL command as

(i) **Data Definition Language (DDL)** DDL is used to define the structure of your tables and other objects in the database. In DBMS, it is used to specify a database schema as a set of definitions (expressed in DDL), In SQL, DDL allows you to create, alter and destroy database objects.

(ii) **Data Manipulation Language (DML)** DML provides various commands used to access and manipulate data in existing database. This manipulation involves inserting data into database tables, retrieving existing data, deleting data from existing tables and modifying existing data.

(iii) **Transaction Control Language (TCL)** TCL is playing an important role in SQL. TCL commands are used to manage transactions in database. These are also used to manage the changes made by DML statements. It allows statements to be grouped together into logical transactions. A transactions is a single unit of work.

(iv) **Data Control Language (DCL)** DCL commands are used to assign security levels in database which involves multiple user setups.

Basically, the DCL command of the SQL language is used to create privileges to allow users access to and manipulation of the database.

20. Differentiate DDL and DML commands of SQL with examples.

Ans. The differences between DDL and DML commands are

DDL	DML
DDL is the abbreviation of Data Definition Language.	DML is the abbreviation of Data Manipulation Language.
It is used to create and modify the structure of database objects in database.	It is used to retrieve, store, modify, delete, insert and update data in database.
DDL commands allow us to perform tasks related to data definition.	DML commands are used to manipulate data.
For example, CREATE, ALTER and DROP commands.	*For example*, SELECT, UPDATE and INSERT commands.

21. Write SQL commands for the question from (i) to (viii) on the basis of table MASTER (contains details of employees).

Table : MASTER

S.No.	Name	Age	Department	Salary
1	Shyam	21	Computer	12000
2	Shiv	25	Maths	15000
3	Rakesh	31	Hindi	14000
4	Sharmila	32	History	20000
5	Dushyant	25	Software	30000

(i) Write a command to update the salary of the employee to 40000, whose S. No. is 3.

(ii) Write a query to add a column Date_of_Joining to the table MASTER.

(iii) Select Age, Department of those employees whose salary is greater than 12000.

(iv) List all data of table MASTER.

(v) Write a query to change the data type of a column Name to varchar with size 35.

(vi) Write a command to delete the table MASTER those employees whose name is Rakesh.

(vii) Write a command to update the department of the employee to english, whose name is Dushyant.

(viii) Write a command to delete the table with the structure.

Ans. (i)
```
mysql>UPDATE MASTER SET Salary
      = 40000 WHERE S.No.=3;
```
(ii)
```
mysql>ALTER TABLE MASTER ADD
      Date_of_Joining DATE;
```
(iii)
```
mysql>SELECT Age, Department
      FROM MASTER WHERE Salary>12000;
```
(iv)
```
mysql>SELECT * FROM MASTER;
```
(v)
```
mysql>ALTER TABLE MASTER MODIFY
      Name VARCHAR (35);
```
(vi)
```
mysql>DELETE FROM MASTER WHERE
      Name="Rakesh";
```
(vii)
```
mysql>UPDATE MASTER SET Department
      = "English" WHERE Name = "Dushyant";
```
(viii)
```
mysql>DROP TABLE MASTER;
```

22. Consider the following table named "SBOP" with details of account holders. Write commands of MySQL for (i) to (iv).

Table : SBOP

AccountNo	Name	Balance	DateOfOpen	Transactions
SB-1	Mr. Anil	15000.00	2011-02-24	7
SB-2	Mr. Amit	23567.89	NULL	8
SB-3	Mrs. Sakshi	45000.00	2012-02-04	5
SB-4	Mr. Gopal	23812.35	2013-09-22	NULL
SB-5	Mr. Dennis	63459.80	2009-11-10	15

(i) To display AccountNo, Name and DateOfOpen of account holders having transactions more than 8.

(ii) To display all information of account holders whose transaction value is not mentioned.

(iii) To add another column Address with data type and size as Varchar(25).

(iv) To display the month day with reference to DateOfOpen for all the account holders.

Ans. (i)
```
SELECT AccountNo, Name, DateOfOpen
FROM SBOP WHERE Transactions > 8;
```
(ii)
```
SELECT * FROM SBOP
WHERE Transactions IS NULL;
```
(iii)
```
ALTER TABLE SBOP
ADD Address VARCHAR(25);
```
(iv)
```
SELECT DAYOFMONTH(DateOfOpen),
Name FROM SBOP;
```

Multiple Choice Questions

1. .... commands work with entire database objects.
- (a) DML
- (b) DDL
- (c) TCL
- (d) DCL

2. The time format used in MySQL is
- (a) MM:HH:SS
- (b) HH:MM:SS
- (c) SS:MM:HH
- (d) None of these

3. Which of the following are not features of MySQL?
- (a) Source code cannot be modified.
- (b) Free usage for limited period.
- (c) Cannot be redistributed.
- (d) None of the above

4. What is the maximum number of characters that can be specified for a varchar field?
- (a) 10
- (b) 200
- (c) 100
- (d) 255

5. What is the size in bytes of TINYINT data type?
- (a) 2 Bytes
- (b) 1 Byte
- (c) 10 Bytes
- (d) None of these

Short Answer Type Questions

6. Compare the following commands
(i) DROP
(ii) USE

7. Explain the cross platform working feature of MySQL.

8. A table "T1" comprises of 10 columns and 15 rows .
3 more columns and 2 rows are added. What will be the degree and cardinality of the table now?

9. Manoj wants to create tables to store his transaction details with following columns

Table : Transaction	Table : Product
Tran_ID	Prod_ID
Tran_Date	Prodname
Qty	Price
Rate	
Amount	
Prod_ID	

To make these tables, he got confused in some questons. Help him to clarify these issues.

(i) Identify the primary key of Transaction table.

(ii) Identify the foreign key of Transaction table.

10. Given a table "HouseBuilding" carrying following columns

BuildingID	BName	Registration_No	Locality	PinNo	HoldingNo	Phone	E-mail

(i) Identify the columns that can be candidate keys.
(ii) If BuildingID is selected as primary key, which columns will be alternate keys ?

Long Answer Type Questions

11. Write commands as specified

Neeraj wants to create a database "Library" and create a table " Book" in it.

The columns in the table would be as follows. A sample data is also given

BookID	Bookname	Type	Price	Pub
B01	Astronomy	Science	2000.50	PHI

Write the set of SQL commands for the above.

12. Given two tables Student and Hostel

Table : Student

RollNo	Name	Class	HostelID
1	Sumita	11	H1
2	Anil	12	H2
3	Srinjal	8	H1
4	Laxmi	9	H3

Table : Hostel

HostelID	HostelName	Location
H1	Ganga	Delhi
H2	Yamuna	Mumbai
H3	Saraswati	Kolkata

(i) Identify the primary keys of both the tables.

(ii) Identify the foreign key of Student table.

(iii) What is the hostel name of Srinjal?

13. Differentiate primary key and foreign key.

14. Write the following features

(i) Security (ii) Query language support

(iii) Connectivity

Answers

Multiple Choice Questions

1. (b) *2. (b)* *3. (d)* *4. (d)* *5. (b)*

For Detailed Solutions

Scan the code

Queries in SQL

In this Chapter...

- SQL SELECT Statement
- Eliminating Redundant Data (DISTINCT Keyword)
- SQL WHERE Clause
- Operators in MySQL
- Working with NULL Values
- Changing Data with DML Commands
- Manipulating Data of a Table/Relation
- Restructuring a Table (ALTER TABLE Command)
- DROP TABLE Command

A database query is a piece of code that is sent to a database in order to get information back from the database. It is used as the way of retrieving the information from database.

You can say that **query** is basically a **question** that you ask the database. The result of the query is the information that is returned by the database management system.

Queries are constructed using SQL (Structured Query Language) which resembles a high-level programming language.

SQL SELECT Statement

The most commonly used SQL command is SELECT statement. The SQL SELECT statement is used to query or retrieve data from a table in the database. A query may retrieve information from specified columns or from all of the columns in the table.

The retrieved information is stored in a result table, commonly known as the **result set**. To create a simple SQL SELECT statement, you must specify the column(s) name and the table name. The whole query is called SQL SELECT statement.

Syntax

```
SELECT column_list
FROM table_name;
```

Here, **table_name** is the name of the table from which the information is retrieved and **column_list** includes one or more columns from which data is retrieved.

In SQL, **SELECT** clause is used to list the attributes desired in the result of a query and **FROM** clause is used to list the relations from which such columns are to be extracted.

Some terminologies used in SQL commands are given below

Keyword A keyword refers to a special word that has a special meaning to SQL. Reserved keywords are part of the grammar of the SQL language that is used by SQL server to parse and understand the SQL statements.

For example, SELECT, FROM, INSERT, etc., are keywords.

Commands or Statements These are instructions given by you to a SQL database.

For example, `SELECT student_name FROM student;` is a statement.

Clause Commands consist of one or more logically distinct parts, called clauses. Clauses begin with a keyword for which they are generally named, and consist of keywords and arguments.

For example, consider the statement

```
SELECT student_name FROM student;
```

Here, 'SELECT student_name' and 'FROM student' are clauses.

Arguments complete or modify the meaning of a clause.

For example, in the above example, 'student' is the argument and FROM is the keyword of FROM clause.

Selecting Specific Columns

To select any specific column or information from the table, we use the following command

Syntax

```
SELECT<column_name1>,[<column_name2>,…,<column_nameN>]
FROM <table_name>;
```

column_name1,column_name2,…..,column_nameN specifies the name of the columns.

table_name specifies the name of the table from which the data is fetched out.

For example,

Let us consider the following table COMPANY

EMP_ CODE	EMP_ NAME	EMP_ADDRESS	EMP_SALARY	EMP_DEPT_NO	DOJ
100	Rahul Sharma	C-21, Arya Nagar	25600	D05	2012-02-06
101	Vikas Mittal	A/44, Mayur Vihar	26000	D03	2002-12-04
102	Puneet Jain	50-MIG, Rohini	21000	D05	2004-08-06
103	Sachin Vats	A-21, Ankur Vihar	23500	D02	2007-09-06
104	Uday Singh	D-34, Indraprasth	26000	D03	2001-07-06
105	Ravi Shukla	45/A, Vivek Nagar	23500	D01	2012-05-06
106	Vinay Rana	120, DDA Colony	24000	D03	2001-02-06

Suppose you want to retrieve only EMP_SALARY and EMP_DEPT_NO from the above table, write the SELECT command as follows.

```
mysql> SELECT EMP_SALARY, EMP_DEPT_NO
       FROM COMPANY;
```

Above query produces the following output

```
+--------------+-------------+
| EMP_SALARY   | EMP_DEPT_NO |
+--------------+-------------+
|       25600  | D05         |
|       26000  | D03         |
|       21000  | D05         |
|       23500  | D02         |
|       26000  | D03         |
|       23500  | D01         |
|       24000  | D03         |
+--------------+-------------+
7 rows in set (0.00 sec)
```

Selecting All Columns

To select all the columns of a table or entire table we can use an asterisk(*) symbol in place of column_name list.

Syntax

```
SELECT <*> FROM <table_name>;
```

For example, to retrieve all columns from the previous table **COMPANY** use the command given below

```
mysql>SELECT * FROM COMPANY;
```

Above query produces the following output

```
+-----------+--------------+------------------+------------+-------------+------------+
| EMP_CODE  | EMP_NAME     | EMP_ADDRESS      | EMP_SALARY | EMP_DEPT_NO |    DOJ     |
+-----------+--------------+------------------+------------+-------------+------------+
|    100    | Rahul Sharma | C-21, Arya Nagar |   25600    |     D05     | 2012-02-06 |
|    101    | Vikas Mittal | A/44, Mayur Vihar|   26000    |     D03     | 2002-12-04 |
|    102    | Puneet Jain  | 50-MIG, Rohini   |   21000    |     D05     | 2004-08-06 |
|    103    | Sachin Vats  | A-21, Ankur Vihar|   23500    |     D02     | 2007-09-06 |
|    104    | Uday Singh   | D-34, Indraprasth|   26000    |     D03     | 2001-07-06 |
|    105    | Ravi Shukla  | 45/A, Vivek Nagar|   23500    |     D01     | 2012-05-06 |
|    106    | Vinay Rana   | 120, DDA Colony  |   24000    |     D03     | 2001-02-06 |
+-----------+--------------+------------------+------------+-------------+------------+
7 rows in set (0.00 sec)
```

Eliminating Redundant Data (DISTINCT Keyword)

When you are working with the SQL SELECT statement, you will more than likely come across duplicate rows when viewing your query results. This duplication can cause various problems depending upon the applications that use the information. This duplication can happen where no primary or unique key constraints exist, or where these constraints have been disabled.

To remove this redundancy, the SQL DISTINCT keyword is used. By using this keyword, you will be able to remove all duplicate rows from your query result. This keyword is used in conjunction with SELECT statement for fetching only unique records.

Syntax

```
SELECT DISTINCT <column_name>
FROM <table_name>;
```

DISTINCT is an optional keyword that needs to precede the columns that are specified in the SELECT clause.

Using DISTINCT, the system will evaluate that data contained in all of the columns as a single unit, on a row per row basis, and will eliminate any duplicates that it find. It will then return the results of the unique rows that will be remaining.

For example, suppose we want to select only the distinct values from the column named **EMP_DEPT_NO** from the **COMPANY** table, we use the following SELECT command for this purpose,

```
mysql> SELECT DISTINCT EMP_DEPT_NO
       FROM COMPANY;
```

Above query produces the following output

```
+-------------+
| EMP_DEPT_NO |
+-------------+
|     D05     |
|     D03     |
|     D02     |
|     D01     |
+-------------+
4 rows in set (0.00 sec)
```

SQL WHERE Clause

The WHERE clause is used when you want to retrieve specific information from a table exluding other irrelevent data.

For example, when you want to see the information about students in class 10th only then you do not need the information about the students in other classes. Retrieving information about all the students would increase the processing time for the query.

So, SQL offers a feature called WHERE clause, which we can use to restrict the data that is retrieved. The condition you provide in the WHERE clause filters the rows retrieved from the table and gives you only those rows which you wanted to see.

WHERE clause can be used along with SELECT, DELETE, UPDATE statements.

When a WHERE clause is present, the database program goes through the entire table one row at a time and examines each row to determine if the given condition is satisfied. If it is satisfied for a row, the row will be displayed in the output.

The **WHERE** command (clause) with **SELECT** command (clause) can retrieve records from a table with some given conditions. As the select query executes, SQL processes one row at a time.

Each time the conditional statement is met (returns true), a row is returned as a result.

Syntax

```
SELECT <column_name>
FROM <table_name> WHERE<condition>;
```

The non-numeric values (string and dates) in the **WHERE** command must be enclosed in single quotes.

For example, suppose we want to retrieve the **EMP_NAME** and **EMP_SALARY** for those who belongs to department number **D05** from the **COMPANY** table.

The following command is used to perform this task

```
mysql> SELECT EMP_NAME, EMP_SALARY
       FROM COMPANY
       WHERE EMP_DEPT_NO = 'D05';
```

Above query produces the following output

```
+---------------+-------------+
|   EMP_NAME    | EMP_SALARY  |
+---------------+-------------+
|  Rahul Sharma |    25600    |
|  Puneet Jain  |    21000    |
+---------------+-------------+
2 rows in set (0.00 sec)
```

Operators in MySQL

MySQL supports different types of operators, some of them are described below

Arithmetic Operators

These operators are used to perform mathematical calculations, such as addition, subtraction, multiplication, division and remainder.

Some most important arithmetic operators used in MySQL are

OPERATOR	DESCRIPTION
+ (Addition)	Add the two arguments together
− (Subtraction)	Subtract the second argument from the first argument
* (Multiplication)	Multiplies the two arguments
/ (Division)	Divide the first argument by the second argument
% (Remainder)	Divide the first argument from the second argument and provides the remainder of that operation

Syntax

```
SELECT <Expression1> <arithmetic operator>
       <Expression2>
    FROM <table_name>
    WHERE <condition>;
```

For example, query to display **EMP_NAME, EMP_DEPT_NO** and 20% of **EMP_SALARY** for each employee for social fund.

```
mysql> SELECT EMP_NAME, EMP_DEPT_NO,
       EMP_SALARY*0.20
       FROM COMPANY;
```

Above query produces the following output

```
+---------------+-------------+-----------------+
|   EMP_NAME    | EMP_DEPT_NO | EMP_SALARY*0.20 |
+---------------+-------------+-----------------+
|  Rahul Sharma |     D05     |      5120       |
|  Vikas Mittal |     D03     |      5200       |
|  Puneet Jain  |     D05     |      4200       |
|  Sachin Vats  |     D02     |      4700       |
|  Uday Singh   |     D03     |      5200       |
|  Ravi Shukla  |     D01     |      4700       |
|  Vinay Rana   |     D03     |      4800       |
+---------------+-------------+-----------------+
7 rows in set (0.00 sec)
```

Arithmetic operators can be implemented through simple SELECT statement without any table. This acts like a function.

For example, SELECT 35*2+5;

Above query produces the following output

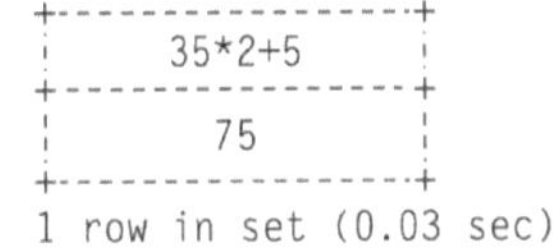

```
+---------+
| 35*2+5  |
+---------+
|   75    |
+---------+
1 row in set (0.03 sec)
```

Comparison Operators

These operators are used to test or compare the value of two operands, *i.e.,* between two variables or between a variable and a constant. If the condition is false, then the result is zero (0) and if the condition is true, then the result is non-zero. These operators are also called **relational operators.**

Some of the comparison/relational operators used in MySQL are as follows

OPERATOR	DESCRIPTION
=	Equal to
>	Greater than
<	Less than
>=	Greater than or equal to
<=	Less than or equal to
<> or !=	Not equal to (not ISO standard)
!<	Not less than (not ISO standard)
!>	Not greater than (not ISO standard)

Syntax

```
SELECT <column name>|*|<expression>
FROM <table name> WHERE<expression>
<comparison operator> <expression>;
```

For example, query to display **EMP_NAME** and **EMP_SALARY** for those employees whose salary is greater than or equal to 25000.

```
mysql> SELECT EMP_NAME,EMP_SALARY
       FROM COMPANY
       WHERE EMP_SALARY> = 25000;
```

Above query produces the following output

```
+---------------+-------------+
| EMP_NAME      | EMP_SALARY  |
+---------------+-------------+
| Rahul Sharma  |    25600    |
| Vikas Mittal  |    26000    |
| Uday Singh    |    26000    |
+---------------+-------------+
3 rows in set (0.00 sec)
```

When we use relational operators with character data type, < means earlier in the alphabet and > means later in the alphabet 'Bangalore '<' 'Brajil' as 'a' comes before 'r' in alphabet.

Logical Operators

The logical operators compare two conditions at a time to determine whether a row can be selected for the output. Logical operators are also called **boolean operators**, because these operators return a boolean data type value as TRUE, or FALSE.

When retrieving data using a SELECT statement, you can use these operators in the WHERE clause, which allows you to combine more than one condition.

Some of the Boolean/Logical operators used in MySQL are as follows

OPERATOR	DESCRIPTION
AND	Logical AND compares two expressions and return true, when both expressions are true
OR	Logical OR compares two expressions and return true, when atleast one of the expressions is true
NOT	NOT takes a single expression as an argument and changes its value from false to true or from true to false. You can use an exclamation point (!) in place of this operator

Syntax

```
SELECT <column name>|*|<expression>
FROM <table name>
WHERE <expressions> <boolean operator>
<expressions>;
```

For example, query to display **EMP_CODE** and **EMP_NAME** for those employees whose **EMP_DEPT_NO** is D05 and **EMP_SALARY** is greater than 22000.

```
mysql> SELECT EMP_CODE,EMP_NAME
       FROM COMPANY
       WHERE (EMP_DEPT_NO='D05'AND
       EMP_SALARY >22000);
```

Above query produces the following output

```
+-----------+---------------+
| EMP_CODE  |   EMP_NAME    |
+-----------+---------------+
|   100     |  Rahul Sharma |
+-----------+---------------+
1 row in set (0.00 sec)
```

For example, query to display **EMP_CODE** and **EMP_NAME** for those employees whose **EMP_DEPT_NO** is D05 or '**EMP_SALARY**' is greater than 22000.

```
mysql> SELECT EMP_CODE, EMP_NAME
       FROM COMPANY
       WHERE(EMP_DEPT_NO = 'D05' OR
       EMP_SALARY>22000);
```

Above query produces the following output

```
+-----------+---------------+
| EMP_CODE  |   EMP_NAME    |
+-----------+---------------+
|   100     |  Rahul Sharma |
|   101     |  Vikas Mittal |
|   102     |  Puneet Jain  |
|   103     |  Sachin Vats  |
|   104     |  Uday Singh   |
|   105     |  Ravi Shukla  |
|   106     |  Vinay Rana   |
+-----------+---------------+
7 rows in set (0.00 sec)
```

For example, query to display **EMP_CODE** and **EMP_NAME** for the employees whose **EMP_SALARY** is not greater than 22000.

```
mysql> SELECT EMP_CODE, EMP_NAME
       FROM COMPANY
       WHERE(NOT EMP_SALARY>22000);
                    or
mysql> SELECT EMP_CODE, EMP_NAME
       FROM COMPANY
       WHERE !(EMP_SALARY>22000);
```

Above query produces the following output

```
+-----------+---------------+
| EMP_CODE  |   EMP_NAME    |
+-----------+---------------+
|   102     |  Puneet Jain  |
+-----------+---------------+
1 row in set (0.00 sec)
```

BETWEEN Operator

The BETWEEN operator is used in a WHERE clause to check that the field values are within a specified inclusive range.

The values can be numbers, text or dates. The range consists of a beginning expression, followed by an **AND** keyword and an end expression.

The operator returns 1 if the search value is present within the range otherwise returns 0. BETWEEN clause is sensitive in order, and the first value in the clause must be first in alphabetic or numeric order.

Syntax

```
SELECT <column name>|*| <expression>
FROM <table name>
WHERE <column name> BETWEEN <value1> AND
<value2>;
```

For example, query to display **EMP_CODE, EMP_NAME** and **EMP_SALARY** for those employees whose salary lies between 23000 to 27000.

```
mysql>SELECT EMP_CODE,EMP_NAME, EMP_SALARY
        FROM COMPANY
        WHERE (EMP_SALARY BETWEEN 23000
        AND 27000);
```

Above query produces the following output

```
+----------+--------------+------------+
| EMP_CODE | EMP_NAME     | EMP_SALARY |
+----------+--------------+------------+
|   100    | Rahul Sharma |   25600    |
|   101    | Vikas Mittal |   26000    |
|   103    | Sachin Vats  |   23500    |
|   104    | Uday Singh   |   26000    |
|   105    | Ravi Shukla  |   23500    |
|   106    | Vinay Rana   |   24000    |
+----------+--------------+------------+
6 rows in set (0.00 sec)
```

IN Operator

This operator checks a value within a set of values separated by commas and retrieve the rows from the table which are matching.

The IN operator returns 1 when the search value is present within the set otherwise returns 0. The IN operator allows you to specify multiple values in a WHERE clause.

Syntax

```
SELECT <column name>|*|<expression>
FROM <table name>
WHERE <column name>IN <(value1, value2,…)>;
```

For example, query to display **EMP_CODE, EMP_NAME** and **DOJ** of the employees whose **EMP_CODE** is 101,104,105.

```
mysql>SELECT EMP_CODE, EMP_NAME, DOJ
        FROM COMPANY
```

```
WHERE EMP_CODE IN (101,104,105);
```

Above query produces the following output

```
+----------+--------------+------------+
| EMP_CODE | EMP_NAME     |    DOJ     |
+----------+--------------+------------+
|   101    | Vikas Mittal | 2002-12-04 |
|   104    | Uday Singh   | 2001-07-06 |
|   105    | Ravi Shukla  | 2012-05-06 |
+----------+--------------+------------+
3 rows in set (0.00 sec)
```

LIKE Operator

This operator is used to search a specified pattern in a column. It is useful when you want to search rows to match a specific pattern, or when you do not know the entire value.

The SQL LIKE clause is used to compare a value to similar values using wildcard operators.

We describe patterns by using two special wildcard operators, given below

(i) **The Percent Sign** (%) It is used to match any substring.

(ii) **The Underscore** (_) It is used to match any character.

The symbols can also be used in combinations.

Syntax

```
SELECT <column name> |*| <expression>
<column name>
FROM <table name>
WHERE <column name> LIKE <pattern>;
```

Here are number of examples showing WHERE clause having different LIKE clause with '%' and '_' operators.

COMMAND	DESCRIPTION
`WHERE SALARY LIKE '100%';`	Find any values that start with 100.
`WHERE SALARY LIKE '%100%';`	Find any values that have 100 in any position.
`WHERE SALARY LIKE '_00%';`	Find any values that have 00 in the second and third positions.
`WHERE SALARY LIKE '1_%_%';`	Find any values that start with 1 and are atleast 2 characters in length.
`WHERE SALARY LIKE '%2';`	Find any values that end with 2.
`WHERE SALARY LIKE '_2%3';`	Find any values that have a 2 in the second position and end with a 3.
`WHERE SALARY LIKE '2_ _3';`	Find any values in a four-digit number that start with 2 and end with 3.

For patterns to include the special pattern characters (that is, % and _), SQL allows the specification of an escape character. The escape character is used immediately before a special pattern character to indicate that the special pattern character is to be treated like a normal character.

We define the escape character for a like comparison using the **escape keyword**.

To illustrate, consider the following patterns, which use a backslash (\ ) as the escape character

Like 'ab\%cd%' escape '\' matches all strings beginning with "ab%cd".

Like 'ab\\cd%' escape '\' matches all strings beginning with "ab\cd".

For example, query to display **EMP_CODE, EMP_NAME** and **EMP_ADDRESS** of the employees whose name started with an alphabet 'V'.

```
mysql> SELECT EMP_CODE,EMP_NAME, EMP_ADDRESS
       FROM COMPANY
       WHERE EMP_NAME LIKE 'V%';
```

Above query produces the following output

```
+----------+-------------+------------------+
| EMP_CODE | EMP_NAME    |   EMP_ADDRESS    |
+----------+-------------+------------------+
|   101    | Vikas Mittal| A/44, Mayur Vihar|
|   106    | Vinay Rana  | 120, DDA Colony  |
+----------+-------------+------------------+
2 rows in set (0.00 sec)
```

Patterns are case-sensitive, that is, upper-case characters do not match with lower-case characters or *vice-versa*.

Operator Precedence

MySQL processes expressions according to a very specific operator precedence. When an expression in an SQL statement is processed, it is evaluated according to the order in which elements are included in the statement and the precedence in which operators are assigned. The operators with higher precedence are evaluated first.

The operator precedences are shown below in the table

PRECEDENCE	OPERATOR	DESCRIPTION
1.	!	Logical Negation
2.	-, ~	Unary minus, Unary bit conversion
3.	^	Bitwise exclusive or operation
4.	*, /, %	Multiplication, Division, Modulus
5.	-, +	Subtraction, Addition
6.	=, < =, >, > =, ! =, LIKE, IN	All comparison operator except BETWEEN
7.	BETWEEN	Between operator
8.	AND, &&	Logical AND operator
9.	OR, II	Logical OR operator
10.	: =	Assignment operator

The operators listed here are shown from the highest precedence to the lowest, *for example,* the arithmetic operators has precedence over the comparison operators. However, operators that appear on the same line of the list have the same level of precedence, so, they are evaluated in the order in which they appear in the expression.

For example, the multiplication (*) and division (/) operators have the same level of precedence so they are evaluated in the order in which they appear.

Working with NULL Values

In MySQL, the empty values are represented as NULL in a table. If a table having null values, then you can display columns with null values or without null values and you can replace NULL values with another value.

To handle NULL values in MySQL, you should use the following commands

IS NULL Clause

If we want to search the column whose value is NULL in a table, then we use IS NULL clause.

Syntax

```
SELECT<column name>|*|<expression>
FROM <table_name>
WHERE <column_name> IS NULL;
```

For example,

Let us consider the following table Teacher

T_No	T_Name	T_Salary	DOJ
T01	Aradhna	17000	2013-01-08
T02	Ritika	NULL	2013-12-14
T03	Ravindra	NULL	2013-11-23
T04	Dushyant	16000	2014-01-10
T05	Swati	19000	2014-02-10

Query to display column whose value is NULL.

```
mysql> SELECT *
       FROM Teacher
       WHERE T_Salary IS NULL;
```

Above query produces the following output

```
+------+----------+----------+------------+
| T_NO | T_NAME   | T_SALARY |    DOJ     |
+------+----------+----------+------------+
| T02  | Ritika   |   NULL   | 2013-12-14 |
| T03  | Ravindra |   NULL   | 2013-11-23 |
+------+----------+----------+------------+
2 rows in set (0.00 sec)
```

IS NOT NULL Clause

If we want to search the column whose value is not NULL in a table then we use IS NOT NULL clause.

Syntax

```
SELECT<column name |*| <expression>
FROM <table_name>
WHERE <column_name> IS NOT NULL;
```

For example,   mysql>SELECT *

```
FROM Teacher
WHERE T_Salary IS NOT NULL;
```

Above query produces the following output

```
+------+----------+----------+------------+
| T_NO | T_NAME   | T_SALARY |    DOJ     |
+------+----------+----------+------------+
| T01  | Aradhna  |  17000   | 2013-01-08 |
| T04  | Dushyant |  16000   | 2014-01-10 |
| T05  | Swati    |  19000   | 2014-02-10 |
+------+----------+----------+------------+
3 rows in set (0.00 sec)
```

IFNULL Function

This function takes two arguments. If the first argument is not equal to NULL, then the function returns the first argument otherwise, the second argument is returned. This function generally used to replace NULL value with another value.

Syntax

```
SELECT <column_name1>, IFNULL
(column_name,"Another value") FROM
<table_name>
WHERE <condition>;
```

For example, mysql>   SELECT T_No, T_Name, IFNULL <T_Salary, 20000> FROM Teacher;
Above query produces the following output

```
+------+----------+------------------------+
| T_NO | T_NAME   | IFNULL<T_Salary,20000> |
+------+----------+------------------------+
| T01  | Aradhna  |         17000          |
| T02  | Ritika   |         20000          |
| T03  | Ravindra |         20000          |
| T04  | Dushyant |         16000          |
| T05  | Swati    |         19000          |
+------+----------+------------------------+
5 rows in set (0.00 sec)
```

The IFNULL () function is available in MySQL, and not in SQL server or Oracle.

Changing Data with DML Commands

DML (Data Manipulation Language) is a category of SQL used to access and manipulate data in existing database. In DML commands, INSERT command is used to insert the data into a table.

Inserting Data

Inserting is a process of adding information into a table. When a table is created, it does not contain any data. Data is inserted in one row at a time.

Inserting a New Row-INSERT INTO Command

The INSERT command is used to add a single record or multiple records into a table.

Syntax

```
INSERT  INTO  <table_name>(col_1,   col_2,
col_3,.., col_n) VALUES(value_1, value_2,...
value_n);
```

Here, table_name defines the name of a table, where data will be inserted. col_1, col_2, col_3,..., col_n are the columns of the current table. value_1, value_2,..., value_n are the data values against each column.

For example, The following information exists in the table STUDENT

```
+---------+--------+----------+
| Roll_No |  Name  | Subject  |
+---------+--------+----------+
|   101   |  Rahul |   Art    |
|   102   |  Vikas | Science  |
|   103   | Puneet | Science  |
|   104   | Sachin |   Art    |
|   105   |  Uday  | Commerce |
+---------+--------+----------+
```

To add a new row into the STUDENT table use the INSERT INTO command as follow

```
mysql>INSERT  INTO  STUDENT(Roll_No,  Name,
Subject) VALUES(106, 'Ajay', 'Science');
```

Now, the table STUDENT will look like as follows

To add a new row into the STUDENT table use the INSERT INTO command as follow

```
mysql>INSERT  INTO  STUDENT(Roll_No,  Name,
Subject) VALUES(106, 'Ajay', 'Science');
```

Now, the table STUDENT will look like as follows

```
+---------+--------+----------+
| Roll_No |  Name  | Subject  |
+---------+--------+----------+
|   101   |  Rahul |   Art    |
|   102   |  Vikas | Science  |
|   103   | Puneet | Science  |
|   104   | Sachin |   Art    |
|   105   |  Uday  | Commerce |
|   106   |  Ajay  | Science  |
+---------+--------+----------+
```

Inserting Null Values

When you execute the INSERT statement, the database server inserts a NULL value into any column for which you provide no value, as well as for all columns that have no default values.

For example,
```
mysql>INSERT INTO STUDENT(Roll_No, Name) VALUES(107, 'Viku');
```
The above command inserts only **Roll_No** and **Name** of the table **STUDENT** but the remaining column **Subject** (as same in previous table) becomes NULL.

You can also specify the NULL Keyword in the VALUES clause to indicate that a column should be assigned a NULL value.

For example,
```
mysql>INSERT INTO STUDENT(Roll_No, Name, Subject) VALUES(107, 'Viku', NULL);
```
Now, the table STUDENT will look like as follows

Roll_No	Name	Subject
101	Rahul	Art
102	Vikas	Science
103	Puneet	Science
104	Sachin	Art
105	Uday	Commerce
106	Ajay	Science
107	Viku	NULL

Inserting Numeric and Character Values

We insert both numeric and character type values in a table. In MySQL, the numeric values are accepted in the data types called INT, SMALLINT, MEDIUMINT, FLOAT, DOUBLE etc., and character data types are accepted in CHAR, VARCHAR etc.

We give the char values in quotes (' ') and numerical values without quotes.

For example,
```
mysql> INSERT INTO STUDENT1(Roll_No, Name, Total, Percentage) VALUES (129,'Vinay', 1560,
70.5);
```
The above command inserts both character and numeric values

Here,   Roll_No Integer value

      Name Character value

      Total Double int value

      Percentage Float value

Output
```
Query OK, 1 row affected <0.03 sec>
```
The column in which a value is not inserted in the above command contains NULL value.

Inserting Date Values

A simple date value in MySQL exists in 'YYYY-MM-DD' format.

For example, first four digits YYYY depicting Year, next two digits MM depicting Month and last two digits DD depicting Date.

For example,
```
mysql> INSERT INTO STUDENT1(Roll_ No, Name, Total, DOB) VALUES(129, 'Vinay', 1560,
'1984-12-29');
```
Output
```
Query OK, 1 row affected <0.03 sec>
```

Manipulating Data of a Table/Relation

UPDATE Command

The UPDATE command is used to update a single record or multiple records in a table. The UPDATE command is used to modify the existing rows in a table. To update multiple fields, each field assignment is separated with a comma(,) symbol.

The WHERE clause in the UPDATE syntax specifies which record or records should be updated. If you omit the WHERE clause, all records will be updated.

Syntax

```
UPDATE<table name > SET <column1> = <value1>, [<column2> - <value2> ,.....]
WHERE <condition>;
```

In above query, update the EMP_SALARY from the given table COMPANY.

```
mysql>UPDATE COMPANY SET EMP_SALARY=28000
      WHERE EMP_CODE=100;
```

To view the output of the above command use SELECT command.

```
mysql>SELECT * FROM COMPANY;
```

Above query produces the following output

EMP_CODE	EMP_NAME	EMP_ADDRESS	EMP_SALARY	EMP_DEPT_NO	DOJ
100	Rahul Sharma	C-21, Arya Nagar	28000	D05	2012-02-06
101	Vikas Mittal	A/44, Mayur Vihar	26000	D03	2002-12-04
102	Puneet Jain	50-MIG, Rohini	21000	D05	2004-08-06
103	Sachin Vats	A-21, Ankur Vihar	23500	D02	2007-09-06
104	Uday Singh	D-34, Indraprasth	26000	D03	2001-07-06
105	Ravi Shukla	45/A, Vivek Nagar	23500	D01	2012-05-06
106	Vinay Rana	120, DDA Colony	24000	D03	2001-02-06

```
7 rows in set (0.00 sec)
```

Using Expressions in Update

Expression are also used in the SET clause of the UPDATE command to manipulate the values.

For example, if you want to increase the salary of each employee by 1000.

Then you could use the following query

```
mysql>UPDATE COMPANY SET EMP_SALARY=EMP_SALARY+1000;
```

To view the output of the above command use SELECT command.

```
mysql>SELECT * FROM COMPANY;
```

Above query produces the following output

EMP_CODE	EMP_NAME	EMP_ADDRESS	EMP_SALARY	EMP_DEPT_NO	DOJ
100	Rahul Sharma	C-21, Arya Nagar	29000	D05	2012-02-06
101	Vikas Mittal	A/44, Mayur Vihar	27000	D03	2002-12-04
102	Puneet Jain	50-MIG, Rohini	22000	D05	2004-08-06
103	Sachin Vats	A-21, Ankur Vihar	24500	D02	2007-09-06
104	Uday Singh	D-34, Indraprasth	27000	D03	2001-07-06
105	Ravi Shukla	45/A, Vivek Nagar	24500	D01	2012-05-06
106	Vinay Rana	120, DDA Colony	25000	D03	2001-02-06

```
7 rows in set (0.00 sec)
```

You can use the WHERE command to update the salary of some employee's, as follows

```
mysql>UPDATE COMPANY
      SET EMP_SALARY = EMP_SALARY + 1000
      WHERE EMP_DEPT_NO = 'D05';
```

To view the output of the above command use SELECT command.

```
mysql>SELECT * FROM COMPANY;
```

Above query produces the following output

```
+----------+--------------+-------------------+------------+-------------+------------+
| EMP_CODE | EMP_NAME     | EMP_ADDRESS       | EMP_SALARY | EMP_DEPT_NO |    DOJ     |
+----------+--------------+-------------------+------------+-------------+------------+
|   100    | Rahul Sharma | C-21, Arya Nagar  |   30000    |    D05      | 2012-02-06 |
|   101    | Vikas Mittal | A/44, Mayur Vihar |   27000    |    D03      | 2002-12-04 |
|   102    | Puneet Jain  | 50-MIG, Rohini    |   23000    |    D05      | 2004-08-06 |
|   103    | Sachin Vats  | A-21, Ankur Vihar |   24500    |    D02      | 2007-09-06 |
|   104    | Uday Singh   | D-34, Indraprasth |   27000    |    D03      | 2001-07-06 |
|   105    | Ravi Shukla  | 45/A, Vivek Nagar |   24500    |    D01      | 2012-05-06 |
|   106    | Vinay Rana   | 120, DDA Colony   |   25000    |    D03      | 2001-02-06 |
+----------+--------------+-------------------+------------+-------------+------------+
7 rows in set (0.00 sec)
```

Updating to NULL Values

You can use UPDATE command to enter the NULL values just as other values. *For example*, the address of the employee Ravi Shukla is changed. But for the time being, the new address is not known, thus NULL value is to be inserted for the address of Ravi Shukla. This can be done as follows

```
mysql>UPDATE COMPANY SET EMP_ADDRESS = NULL
      WHERE EMP_NAME = 'Ravi Shukla';
```

To view the ouput of the above command, use SELECT command

```
mysql>SELECT * FROM COMPANY;
```

Above query produces the following output

```
+----------+--------------+-------------------+------------+-------------+------------+
| EMP_CODE | EMP_NAME     | EMP_ADDRESS       | EMP_SALARY | EMP_DEPT_NO |    DOJ     |
+----------+--------------+-------------------+------------+-------------+------------+
|   100    | Rahul Sharma | C-21, Arya Nagar  |   30000    |    D05      | 2012-02-06 |
|   101    | Vikas Mittal | A/44, Mayur Vihar |   27000    |    D03      | 2002-12-04 |
|   102    | Puneet Jain  | 50-MIG, Rohini    |   23000    |    D05      | 2004-08-06 |
|   103    | Sachin Vats  | A-21, Ankur Vihar |   24500    |    D02      | 2007-09-06 |
|   104    | Uday Singh   | D-34, Indraprasth |   27000    |    D03      | 2001-07-06 |
|   105    | Ravi Shukla  | NULL              |   24500    |    D01      | 2012-05-06 |
|   106    | Vinay Rana   | 120, DDA Colony   |   25000    |    D03      | 2001-02-06 |
+----------+--------------+-------------------+------------+-------------+------------+
7 rows in set (0.00 sec)
```

DELETE Command

To discard unwanted data from a database, the DELETE command is used. The DELETE command uses a WHERE clause. If you don't use a WHERE clause, all rows in the table will be deleted.

Syntax `DELETE FROM <table name> WHERE <condition>;`

For example, query to delete the record of employee Puneet Jain from the table COMPANY.

```
mysql> DELETE FROM COMPANY WHERE EMP_NAME ='Puneet Jain';
```

To view the output of the above command use SELECT command.

```
mysql>SELECT * FROM COMPANY;
```

Now, above query produces the following output

```
+----------+--------------+-------------------+------------+-------------+------------+
| EMP_CODE | EMP_NAME     | EMP_ADDRESS       | EMP_SALARY | EMP_DEPT_NO |    DOJ     |
+----------+--------------+-------------------+------------+-------------+------------+
|   100    | Rahul Sharma | C-21, Arya Nagar  |   30000    |    D05      | 2012-02-06 |
|   101    | Vikas Mittal | A/44, Mayur Vihar |   27000    |    D03      | 2002-12-04 |
|   103    | Sachin Vats  | A-21, Ankur Vihar |   24500    |    D02      | 2007-09-06 |
|   104    | Uday Singh   | D-34, Indraprasth |   27000    |    D03      | 2001-07-06 |
|   105    | Ravi Shukla  | NULL              |   24500    |    D01      | 2012-05-06 |
|   106    | Vinay Rana   | 120, DDA Colony   |   25000    |    D03      | 2001-02-06 |
+----------+--------------+-------------------+------------+-------------+------------+
6 rows in set (0.00 sec)
```

Delete All Rows

To delete all rows in a table without deleting the table structure, the following command is used

Syntax `DELETE FROM <table name>;`
or `DELETE * FROM <table name>;`

It is very easy to drop an existing MySQL table, but you need to be very careful while deleting any existing table because data lost will not be recovered after deleting a table.

Restructuring a Table (ALTER TABLE Command)

One can change the structure of a table after creating it, by using ALTER command. To restructure a table either by adding new columns or deleting existing columns, the ALTER command is used. It is also used to modify the structure of a table by modifying the definition of its columns.

The ALTER command is used to perform the following functions

Adding a Column in a Table

Syntax `ALTER TABLE <table_name> ADD <column_name> datatype <value>;`

For example, query to add a column named "EXPERIENCE" of data type INT of size 3 to the table COMPANY used in above section. `mysql>ALTER TABLE COMPANY ADD EXPERIENCE INT(3);`

To view the output of the above command use SELECT command.

```
mysql>SELECT * FROM COMPANY;
```

Now, above query produces the following output

EMP_CODE	EMP_NAME	EMP_ADDRESS	EMP_SALARY	EMP_DEPT_NO	DOJ	EXPERIENCE
100	Rahul Sharma	C-21, Arya Nagar	30000	D05	2012-02-06	NULL
101	Vikas Mittal	A/44, Mayur Vihar	27000	D03	2002-12-04	NULL
103	Sachin Vats	A-21, Ankur Vihar	24500	D02	2007-09-06	NULL
104	Uday Singh	D-34, Indraprasth	27000	D03	2001-07-06	NULL
105	Ravi Shukla	NULL	24500	D01	2012-05-06	NULL
106	Vinay Rana	120, DDA Colony	25000	D03	2001-02-06	NULL

```
6 rows in set (0.00 sec)
```

Deleting a Column from a Table

Syntax `ALTER TABLE<table_name> DROP COLUMN<column_name>;`
or `ALTER TABLE<table_name> DROP <column_name>;`

For example, query to drop a column name "EXPERIENCE" from the table COMPANY.

```
mysql>ALTER TABLE COMPANY DROP COLUMN EXPERIENCE;
```

To view the output of the above command use SELECT command.

```
mysql>SELECT * FROM COMPANY;
```

Now, above query produces the following output

EMP_CODE	EMP_NAME	EMP_ADDRESS	EMP_SALARY	EMP_DEPT_NO	DOJ
100	Rahul Sharma	C-21, Arya Nagar	30000	D05	2012-02-06
101	Vikas Mittal	A/44, Mayur Vihar	27000	D03	2002-12-04
103	Sachin Vats	A-21, Ankur Vihar	24500	D02	2007-09-06
104	Uday Singh	D-34, Indraprasth	27000	D03	2001-07-06
105	Ravi Shukla	45/A, Vivek Nagar	24500	D01	2012-05-06
106	Vinay Rana	120, DDA Colony	25000	D03	2001-02-06

```
6 rows in set (0.00 sec)
```

Changing the Data Type of a Column in a Table

Syntax `ALTER TABLE <table_name> MODIFY COLUMN <column_name> datatype<value>;`
or `ALTER TABLE <table_name> MODIFY <column_name> datatype<value>;`

For example, query to change the data type of a column DOJ to datatype VARCHAR (15) from the table COMPANY used in above section.

```
mysql>ALTER TABLE COMPANY MODIFY COLUMN DOJ
VARCHAR (15);
```

Above query produce a following output

```
+----------------------------------------------+
| Query OK, 6 rows  affected (0.17 sec)        |
| Records : 6 Duplicates : 0 Warnings : 0      |
+----------------------------------------------+
```

Add and Drop Constraints

Syntax

To ADD PRIMARY KEY or UNIQUE KEY constraint

```
ALTER TABLE table_name
ADD CONSTRAINT <constraint_name>
PRIMARY KEY/UNIQUE KEY <column_name>;
```

To ADD FOREIGN KEY constraint

```
ALTER TABLE table_name
ADD CONSTRAINT <constraint_name>
FOREIGN KEY(col1, col2,..., coln)
REFERENCES <parent_table>(col1,
col2,...,coln);
```

To ADD CHECK constraint

```
ALTER TABLE table_name
ADD CONSTRAINT <constraint_name> CHECK
(column_name condition);
```

To DROP constraints

```
ALTER TABLE table_name
DROP CONSTRAINT constraint_name;
```

For example, To add primary key constraint employee_pk in EMPLOYEE table.

```
ALTER TABLE EMPLOYEE ADD CONSTRAINT
employee_pk PRIMARY KEY(emp_id);
```

For example, To drop a constraint chk_person from table PERSONS.

```
ALTER TABLE PERSONS
DROP CONSTRAINT chk_Persons;
```

Disable and Enable Constraints

Syntax To DISABLE constraints

```
ALTER TABLE table_name
DISABLE CONSTRAINT constraint_name;
```

To Enable constraints

```
ALTER TABLE table_name
ENABLE CONSTRAINT constraint_name;
```

For example, To disable a foreign key constraint employee_fk from EMPLOYEE table.

```
ALTER TABLE EMPLOYEE
DISABLE CONSTRAINT employee_fk;
```

For example, To enable a primary key constraint employee_pk from EMPLOYEE table.

```
ALTER TABLE EMPLOYEE
ENABLE CONSTRAINT employee_pk;
```

RENAME Command   The RENAME command is used to change the name of the table or the database object.

Syntax
```
RENAME table oldtable_name TO
    newtable_name;
```

For example, To rename the STUDENT table as my_students.

```
RENAME table STUDENT TO  my_students;
```

DROP TABLE Command

SQL DROP TABLE statement is used to remove table in a database. When you use the SQL DROP TABLE statement to remove a table, the database deletes all objects.

Syntax
```
DROP TABLE table_name;
```

Here, table_name is the name of table to be deleted.

ORDER BY Clause

The ORDER BY keyword is used to sort the result set along a specified column with the SELECT command. The ORDER BY keyword sorts the records in ascending order by default. If you want to sort the records in a descending order, you can use the DESC keyword.

Syntax
```
SELECT column_name(s)
FROM table_name
ORDER BY column_name(s)ASC/DESC;
```

e.g. If we have the following PERSONS table

P_Id	LastName	FirstName	Address	City
1	Hansen	Ola	Timoteivn 10	Sandnes
2	Svendson	Tove	Borgvn 23	Sandnes
3	Pettersen	Kari	Storgt 20	Stavanger

and we want to sort the persons by their last name in ascending order.

We use the following SELECT statement

```
SELECT * FROM PERSONS
ORDER BY LastName ASC;
```

The result set will look like this

P_Id	LastName	FirstName	Address	City
1	Hansen	Ola	Timoteivn 10	Sandnes
3	Pettersen	Kari	Storgt 20	Stavanger
2	Svendson	Tove	Borgvn 23	Sandnes

Chapter Practice

Objective Questions

• Multiple Choice Questions

1. The clause used to check NULL values is
(a) IS NULL
(b) IS NOT NULL
(c) Both (a) and (b)
(d) None of these

Ans. (a) The IS NULL clause is used to check NULL values in a field.

2. The .... operator is used for pattern matching.
(a) BETWEEN
(b) LIKE
(c) IN
(d) LOOKSLIKE

Ans. (b) The LIKE operator is used to match patterns in a field.

3. The two characters used for pattern matching using LIKE operator are
(a) _ , * (b) * , / (c) // , / (d) %, _

Ans. (d) The %, _ are the two characters used for pattern matching of values in a column.

4. The clause used to specify a condition in a query is
(a) MATCH
(b) WHOSE
(c) WHERE
(d) None of these

Ans. (c) The WHERE clause is used to specify a condition in a query.

5. To delete all the records from a table "Product" the command will be
(a) `DEL FROM Product;`
(b) `DELETE FROM Product;`
(c) `REMOVE ALL FROM Product;`
(d) `DELETE All;`

Ans. (b) To delete all the records from a table "Product" the command will be
`DELETE FROM product;`

6. The .... character displays all the columns of a table in a SELECT query.
(a) #
(b) @
(c) *
(d) /

Ans. (c) The * character displays all the columns in a SELECT query.

7. The .... command removes a table completely.
(a) DELETE
(b) REMOVE
(c) DROP
(d) UPDATE

Ans. (c) The DROP command removes a table completely along with its data.

8. The "SET" clause is used along with .... command.
(a) DELETE
(b) DESCRIBE
(c) CREATE
(d) UPDATE

Ans. (d) The UPDATE command updates data of a table . It uses the "SET" clause to specify the field to be updated.

9. What is true about the following SQL statement?
`mysql> SELECT*FROM Student;`   **(NCERT)**
(a) Displays contents of table 'Student'.
(b) Displays column names and contents of table 'Student'.
(c) Results in error as improper case has been used.
(d) Displays only the column names of table 'Student'.

Ans. (b) The command displays entire contents of the table along with column names.

10. What will be the output of following query?

```
INSERT INTO Student                (NCERT)
VALUES ("Suhana",109,'F'),
VALUES ("Rivaan",102,'M'),
VALUES ("Atharv",103,'M'),
VALUES ("Rishika",105,'F'),
VALUES ("Garvit",104,'M'),
VALUES ("Shaurya",109,'M');
```
(a) Error
(b) No Error
(c) Depends on compiler
(d) Successful completion of the query

Ans. (a) Multiple values cannot be inserted in a single INSERT command.

11. Which function is used to replace NULL value with another value?
(a) IFNULL
(b) IS NULL
(c) IS NOT NULL
(d) None of these

Ans. (a) IFNULL function is used to replace NULL value with another value.

12. Which operator is used to compare a value to a specified list of values?

(a) ANY (b) BETWEEN
(c) ALL (d) IN

Ans. (d) The IN operator easily tests the expression, if it matches any value in a specified list of value.

13. If we have not specified ASC or DESC after a SQL ORDER By clause, the following is used by default

(a) DESC (b) ASC
(c) There is no default value (d) None of these

Ans. (b) If we have not specified any sorting with the ORDER By clause. SQL always uses the ASC as a default sorting order.

14. Which of the following is the correct order of a SQL statement?

(a) SELECT, GROUP By, WHERE, HAVING
(b) SELECT, WHERE, GROUP BY, HAVING
(c) SELECT, HAVING, WHERE, GROUP BY
(d) SELECT, WHERE, HAVING, GROUP BY

Ans. (b) In SQL statement, the WHERE clause always comes before GROUP BY and HAVING clause always comes after GROUP BY. Hence, option (b) is correct.

• Case Based MCQs

Direction *Read the case and answer the following questions.*

15. Ronita wants to store the data of some products in a table as follows

PNo	PName	Qty	Date_Of_Mfg
P01	Pencil	20	2020-09-01
P02	Eraser	5	1990-09-11
P03	Book	16	2000-04-03
P04	Notebook	15	2016-12-11
P05	Color	10	2015-02-04

She also wants to perform some operations and manipulations on the table . Help her to find the solutions of following questions

(i) A command that displays the details of all the products will be

(a) `SELECT * FROM Product;`
(b) `SHOW * FROM Product;`
(c) `DISPLAY * FROM Product;`
(d) `SELECT ALL details FROM Product;`

(ii) The default date format in which date has to be stored in MySQL is

(a) DD-MM-YYYY (b) DD-YY-MM
(c) MM-YY-DD (d) YYYY-MM-DD

(iii) Which command she can use to add a new column to the table?

(a) INSERT (b) UPDATE
(c) ADD COLUMN (d) ALTER

(iv) Suggest her a proper data type for the "PName" column.

(a) Varchar
(b) Double
(c) Float
(d) Integer

(v) She is confused whether she has to use the "COLUMN" clause with the ALTER TABLE command to add a column to the table. What should she do ?

(a) COLUMN clause is must.
(b) COLUMN clause is optional.
(c) COLUMN clause is must for adding integer columns only.
(d) None of the above

Ans. (i) (a) `SELECT * FROM Product;`
(ii) (d) By default, MySQL stores date in YYYY-MM-DD format.
(iii) (d) The ALTER command can be used to make any changes to the structure of a table.
(iv) (a) The varchar is a variable length data type that can used for columns storing string/character type of data.
(v) (b) With the ALTER TABLE command the COLUMN clause is optional, in adding columns to a table.

16. Sonali wants to perform certain operations on a table "Exam" storing exam details . She is not sure about some of the commands and is getting errors.

Help her in proper execution of her operations.

Exam_ID	ExamName	MaxMarks	PassMarks
E01	HalfYearly	45	14.0
E02	Term-I	35	10.5
E03	PreBoard	50	15.0
E04	UnitTest	20	7.0
E05	Term-II	35	10.5

(i) The command she should write to increase the PassMarks by 5 will be

(a) `UPDATE Exam SET PassMarks=5;`
(b) `UPDATE Exam SET PassMarks+5;`
(c) `UPDATE Exam SET PassMarks= PassMarks+5;`
(d) `UPDATE Exam SET PassMarks= PassMarks+5`

(ii) She wants to add a new column "NegativeMarks" of type integer. She wrote the following command. What is the error?

`ALTER Exam ADD NegativeMarks integer;`

(a) Command cannot have ; at the end.
(b) Command is missing "TABLE" clause after "ALTER".
(c) Command has to be written in uppercase.
(d) The "COLUMN" clause has to be added after "ADD"

(iii) What data type she has to use for the "PassMarks" column?

(a) Integer (b) Float
(c) String (d) Char

(iv) She is confused whether she has to use DELETE or DROP command for deleting all data of the table keeping the structure. Which command she has to use?
   (a) DELETE   (b) DROP
   (c) Any of (a) or (b)   (d) None of these

(v) Can she add another ExamID as "E05"? Assuming Exam ID is primary key of table
   (a) Yes   (b) No
   (c) Yes , if other values are NULL.
   (d) None of these

Ans. (i) (*d*) The UPDATE command updates data of table and the modifying field can be set to a value or expression.

(ii) (*b*) The actual command will be
```
ALTER TABLE Exam ADD NegativeMarks
integer;
```

(iii) (*b*) The "PassMarks" column stores fractional values , hence the data type should be float.

(iv) (*a*) The DELETE command can be used to delete all the records from table Exam.

(v) (*b*) ExamID is the primary key of the table, so it cannot have duplicate values.

PART 2
Subjective Questions

• Short Answer Type Questions

1. Differentiate between ALTER and UPDATE commands in SQL. **(NCERT)**

Ans.

ALTER command	UPDATE command
It belongs to DDL category.	It belongs to DML category.
It changes the structure of the table.	It modifies data of the table.
Columns can be added, modified , deleted etc.	Data can be changed, updated with values and expressions.

2. How is char data type different from varchar data type? **(NCERT)**

Ans.

Char	Varchar
It is fixed length.	It is variable length.
Wastage of memory.	Memory usage only as per data size.
Less useful.	Better data type.

3. Explain the use of ORDER BY clause.

Ans. The ORDER BY clause is used to arrange the records in ascending or descending order. Data present in a table can be arranged as per requirement on a specific field in ascending or descending order. The default is ascending order. To arrange in descending order the DESC clause is to be used. To arrange in ascending order ASC may be used.

e.g. `SELECT * FROM Employee ORDER BY EMP_SALARY DESC;`
The above command arranges the records in descending order of salary.

4. What is the use of AS keyword with SELECT statement?

Ans. In MySQL, the AS keyword is used to temporarily rename the column's name, i.e. the AS keyword is used to define the column alias. This renaming is a temporary change and the actual column name does not change in the database.

5. Name two wildcard characters used in conjunction with the LIKE operator.

Ans. Two wildcard characters used in conjunction with the LIKE operator are given below :
(i) Per cent sign (%) for matching any substring.
(ii) Underscore sign (_) for matching a single character.

6. Write the queries for the following questions using the table Product with the following fields.
(P_ Code, P_Name, Qty, Price)
(i) Display the price of product having code as P06.
(ii) Display the name of all products with quantity greater than 50 and price less than 500.

Ans. (i) `SELECT Price FROM Product WHERE P_Code="P06";`
The criteria of the records that are to be displayed can be specified with WHERE clause of SQL.

(ii) `SELECT P_Name FROM Product WHERE Qty>50 AND Price<500;`
The criteria of the records that are to be displayed can be specified with WHERE clause of SQL. Here, the condition is quantity > 50 and price<500 .

7. Is it compulsory to provide values for all columns of a table while adding records? Give an example.

Ans. No it is not compulsory to provide values for all columns of a table while adding records. We can use NULL values wherever values are missing.

e.g. `INSERT INTO Employee VALUES (1,NULL,"Sales",89000);`

8. Amit wrote the command to create a table "Student" as :
```
CREATE TABLE Student(RollNo integer,
Name varchar(20), Marks float(8,2));
```
What does (8,2) mean here?

Ans. While specifying float columns in a table the width and the number of decimals have to be specified. Here 8 is the total width and 2 is the number of decimal places for the Marks column.

9. Rakesh wants to increase the price of some of the products by 20% , of his store whose price is less than 200. Assuming the following structure , what will be the query?

PNo	PName	Quality	Price

Ans.
```
UPDATE ITEM SET Price=Price + Price *
0.2 WHERE Price<200 ;
```
The UPDATE command updates data of a table . While updating, the expression for update value can be assigned to the updating field. The records to be updated can be specified as WHERE condition.

10. Write the use of LIKE clause and a short explanation on the two characters used with it.

Ans. This operator is used to search a specified pattern in a column. It is useful when you want to search rows to match a specific pattern or when you do not know the entire value. The SQL LIKE clause is used to compare a value to similar values using wildcard characters.

We describe patterns by using two special wildcard characters, given below:

(i) The per cent sign (%) is used to match any substring.

(ii) The underscore (_) is used to match any single character. The symbols can also be used in combinations.

11. Given the command below.

DELETE FROM Toys WHERE ToyName LIKE "S_t%";

Which records will be deleted by the above command?

Ans. The command has a LIKE clause with "S_t%" which means all the toy names that start with the letter 'S' and has 3rd letter as 't' will deleted.

12. In the following query how many rows will be deleted?   **(NCERT)**
```
DELETE Student
WHERE Student_ID=109;
```
(Assuming a Student table with primary key Student_ID)

Ans.
```
DELETE FROM Student WHERE
Student_ID=109;
```
Here, the "FROM" clause is missing , so the command will produce an error.

13. If the value in the column is repeatable, how do you find out the unique values?   **(NCERT)**

Ans. The DISTINCT clause in SQL is used to display only distinct values in a column of a table. Hence, if the column allows duplicate values the unique values can be extracted using the DISTINCT clause.
```
SELECT DISTINCT CLASS FROM Student ;
```
This displays only the unique classes.

14. What do you mean by an operator? Name any four operators used in queries.

Ans. An operator is a component of an expression that represents the action that should be taken over a set of values.

Four operators used in queries are

(i) Arithmetic operators

(ii) Comparison operators

(iii) Boolean/Logical operators

(iv) Between operator

15. How NOT operator is used with WHERE clause? Give an example.

Ans. The WHERE clause is used to retrieve some given data according to the condition and NOT operator reverses the result of it.

For example,
```
mysql>SELECT Name, Class, Games FROM
Student_table WHERE NOT Games = 'FootBALL';
```

16. Consider the following table with their fields.
```
EMPLOYEE (E_CODE, E_NAME, DESIG, SALARY,
                                      DOJ)
```
List the names, salary, PF, HRA, DA of all the employees in the EMPLOYEE Table. HRA is 25% of salary, DA is 10% of salary and PF is 5% of salary. The result should be in descending order of salary.

Ans. mysql>SELECT E_NAME, SALARY, SALARY *0.25 AS HRA, SALARY * 0.10 AS DA,
```
        SALARY *0.05 AS PF
        FROM EMPLOYEE
        ORDER BY SALARY DESC;
```

17. What are the functions of ALTER TABLE command?

Ans. The main functions of ALTER TABLE command are

(i) Add or drop columns.

(ii) Change the column definition of a column.

(iii) Add or drop constraint.

(iv) Rename a column.

18. Write syntax of the conditions given below.

(i) Add a column in a table.

(ii) Delete a column from a table.

Ans. (i) ALTER TABLE<table_name>ADD <column_name>datatype<value>;

(ii) ALTER TABLE<table_name>DROP COLUMN<column_name>;

19. Consider the following table PREPAID. Write MySQL commands for the statements given below.

S_No	C_Name	Model	Connection
1.	Sita	Nokia	Airtel
2.	Geeta	Samsung	Idea
3.	Ritesh	LG	BSNL
4.	Jayant	Micromax	Reliance

(i) DELETE a column name Model.

(ii) DELETE a customer record where connection type is BSNL.

Ans. (i) mysql> ALTER TABLE PREPAID DROP Model;

(ii) mysql> DELETE FROM PREPAID WHERE Connection = 'BSNL';

20. Is it possible to disable a constraint? Give reasons in support of your answer.

Ans. Yes, we can disable a constraint using keyword DISABLE.
```
ALTER TABLE table_name
DISABLE CONSTRAINT constraint_name;
```

21. Sarthak, a student of class XII, created a table "CLASS". Grade is one of the columns of this table. To find the details of students whose Grades have not been entered. He wrote the following MySQL query, which did not give the desired result?

```
SELECT * FROM CLASS WHERE Grade = "Null";
```

Help Sarthak to run the query by removing the errors from the query and write the correct query.

Ans. Query to find the details of students whose Grade have not been entered:

```
SELECT * FROM CLASS WHERE Grade IS NULL;
```

22. Define UPDATE command of MySQL with its basic syntax and also give one of its example.

Ans. An UPDATE command is used to directly change or modify the values stored in one or more fields in a specified record.

Syntax,

```
UPDATE<table_name>SET[<column1>=<value  1>,
<column 2>= <value 2>.....]
Where <condition>;
```

For example,
Consider the given table PREPAID in above question.
mysql>UPDATE PREPAID SET Model = 'Sony' WHERE S_No=2;

23. What will be the output of the following queries on the basis of EMPLOYEE table?

Table: EMPLOYEE

Emp_Id	Name	Salary
E01	Siya	54000
E02	Joy	NULL
E03	Allen	32000
E04	Neev	42000

(i) SELECT Salary + 100 FROM EMPLOYEE WHERE Emp_Id = 'E02';

(ii) SELECT Name FROM EMPLOYEE WHERE Emp_Id = 'E04';

Ans. The output of the following queries

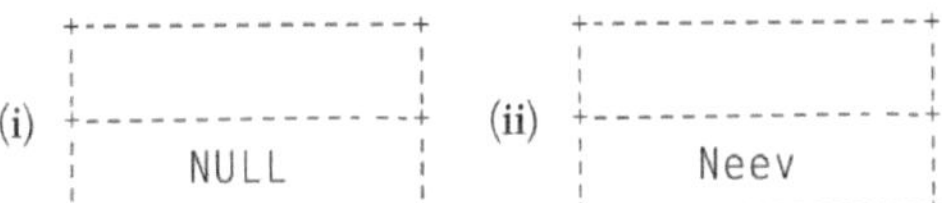

• Long Answer Type Questions

24. Consider the table Hospital storing details of patients as follows

Table : Hospital

PatId	PName	Dept	Charges	DtofAdm
P1	Varun	PAED	700	2021-09-02
P2	Sunita	PAED	900	NULL
P3	Samarpan	ENT	1000	2020-08-09
P4	Rishabh	ORTHO	500	1995-06-05
P5	Bineeta	ORTHO	450	2012-03-04

Write SQL commands for (i) to (iv).

(i) To create the table with appropriate data types.

(ii) To display only the names and departments of patients of "ENT".

(iii) To increase the charges of all departments by 20%.

(iv) To add a new column Phone of type integer.

Ans. (i)
```
CREATE  TABLE  Hospital(PatId  char(5),
Pname  varchar(30),  Dept  varchar(20),
Charges int, DtofAdm Date);
```
(ii)
```
SELECT  PName,  Dept  FROM  Hospital  WHERE
Dept = "ENT";
```
(iii)
```
UPDATE  Hospital  SET  Charges  =  Charges  +
Charges * 0.2;
```
(iv)
```
ALTER TABLE Hospital ADD Phone integer;
```

25. With respect to the table "Toys" write SQL commands to perform the following

ToyID	ToyName	Price	Type
T01	Doll	520	Girls
T02	Video Game	200	Boys
T03	Gun	1600	Boys
T04	Anabelle	1000	Girls
T05	Hot wheels	100	Boys

(i) To add a record "T06,Toy Train,900,Boys" into the table.

(ii) To display ToyName and Price for all toys.

(iii) To display only toynames whose price is greater than 1000.

(iv) To add a column "Quantity" of type int to store quantities of toys.

Ans. (i)
```
INSERT  INTO  Toys  VALUES("T06",  "Toy
Train", 900, "Boys");
```
(ii)
```
SELECT Toyname, Price FROM Toys;
```
(iii)
```
SELECT  Toyname  FROM  Toys  WHERE
price>1000;
```
(iv)
```
ALTER TABLE Toys ADD Quantity integer;
```

26. Explain different DML commands with one example of each.

Ans. DML stands for Data Manipulation Language DML commands are those that work with the data and records of a table.

Assuming a table structure as follows

Table : Movie

MovieID	Mname	Type	Cost

Commands :

(i) **SELECT** The SELECT command displays the records of a table with or without conditions.

e.g. To display details of all movies.

```
SELECT * FROM Movie;
SELECT Mname, Cost FROM Movie WHERE
Cost > 100000;
```

(ii) **UPDATE** The UPDATE command updates or modifies the data of a table by a value or expression.

e.g. To increase cost of all movies by 1000.

```
UPDATE Movie SET Cost=cost+1000;
```

(iii) **DELETE** The DELETE command is used to delete records from a table.

e.g. To delete all the records of the table.

```
DELETE FROM Movie;
```

or Delete the records of movie Type "Fiction".

```
DELETE      FROM     Movie      WHERE
Type="Fiction";
```

(iv) **INSERT INTO** The INSERT INTO command is used to insert / add records to a table.

e.g. To add a new record to the table.

```
INSERT INTO Movie VALUES("M01",
"Enter the Dragon","Action",2500000);
```

27. Write SQL queries with respect to the Movie table given below   (NCERT)

Table : Movie

Movie ID	Movie Name	Category	Release Date	Production Cost	Business Cost
001	Hindi_ Movie	Musical	2018-04-23	124500	130000
002	Tamil_ Movie	Action	2016-05-17	112000	118000
003	English_ Movie	Horror	2017-08-06	245000	360000
004	Bengali_ Movie	Adventure	2017-08-04	72000	100000
005	Telugu_ Movie	Action	-	100000	-
006	Punjabi_ Movie	Comedy	-	30500	-

(i) Retrieve movie information without mentioning their column names.

(ii) List business done by the movies showing only MovieID, MovieName and Business Cost.

(iii) List the different categories of movies.

(iv) Find **net profit** of each movie showing its ID, Name and NetProfit.

Ans. (i)
```
SELECT * FROM Movie;
```
The * operator consider all the columns of a table while displaying records with SELECT command.

(ii)
```
SELECT MovieID,MovieName,BusinessCost
FROM Movie;
```

The SELECT command when used with the column list, it displays only the specified columns.

(iii)
```
SELECT DISTINCT Category FROM Movie;
```
The DISTINCT clause extracts unique values from a column of a table.

(iv)
```
SELECT MovieID, MovieName,
BusinessCost-ProductionCost AS "
NetProfit" FROM Movie;
```
Columns along with the calculated columns can be specified with the SELECT command to display them, where the expression of calculation can be specified in the field list.

28. Explain the use of the following clauses

(i) BETWEEN

(ii) ORDER BY

(iii) DISTINCT

(iv) LIKE

Ans. (i) **BETWEEN** The BETWEEN clause is used to specify ranges in a query. The values can be numbers, text or dates. The range consists of a beginning expression, followed by an AND keyword and an end expression.

For example, The command to displays the details of employees whose salary lies between 10000 and 20000.
```
SELECT*FROM Employee WHERE Sal
BETWEEN 10000 AND 20000;
```

(ii) **ORDER BY** The ORDER BY clause is used to arrange the records in ascending or descending order. The clauses ASC and DESC are used to specify ascending or descending.

For example, The command to arrange the records of Employee table in descending order of names.
```
SELECT * FROM Employee ORDER BY Name
DESC;
```

(iii) **DISTINCT** The DISTINCT clause lists only the unique values in a field.

For example, The command to displays only the different departments in the Employee table.
```
SELECT DISTINCT Dept FROM Employee;
```

(iv) **LIKE** The LIKE clause is used for pattern matching in SQL.

For example, The command to displays the details of employees whose name starts with "S".
```
SELECT*FROM Employee WHERE Ename LIKE
"S%",
```

29. Write SQL commands for the questions from (i) to (iv) on the basis of table SHOP.

S_No	P_Name	S_Name	Qty	Cost	City
S1	Biscuit	Priyagold	120	12.00	Delhi
S2	Bread	Britannia	200	25.00	Mumbai
S3	Chocolate	Cadbury	350	40.00	Mumbai
S4	Sauce	Kissan	400	45.00	Chennai

(i) Display all products whose quantity is between 100 and 400.

(ii) Display data for all products sorted by their quantity.

(iii) To list S_Name, P_Name, Cost for all the products whose quantity is less than 300.

(iv) To display S_No, P_Name, S_Name, Qty in descending order of quantity from the SHOP table.

Ans. (i) `mysql> SELECT * FROM SHOP WHERE Qty BETWEEN 100 AND 400;`

(ii) `mysql> SELECT * FROM SHOP ORDER BY Qty;`

(iii) `mysql> SELECT S_Name, P_Name, Cost FROM SHOP WHERE Qty<300;`

(iv) `mysql> SELECT S_No, P_Name, S_Name, Qty FROM SHOP ORDER BY Qty DESC;`

30. Consider the table STUDENT given below and write SQL commands for (i) to (iv).

Student_No	Class	Name	Game	G_Grade	Section	Marks
01	7	Rahul	Swimming	B	A	99
02	8	Sameer	Tenis	A	B	20
03	10	Dushyant	FootBall	C	C	87
04	12	Kapil	Tennis	D	C	90
05	6	Ravinder	Cricket	A	B	97

(i) Display Student_No and G_Grade of all students from table STUDENT.

(ii) List the Name from table STUDENT whose Student _No is 04 or 05 or 02.

(iii) Display Game and Marks for those students whose name starts with alphabet 'D'.

(iv) Write a query to display Name and Section for those students whose Marks lies between 85 to 100.

Ans. (i) `mysql>SELECT Student_No, G_Grade FROM STUDENT;`

(ii) `mysql>SELECT Name FROM STUDENT WHERE Student _No IN (04, 05, 02);`

(iii) `mysql>SELECT Game, Marks FROM STUDENT WHERE Name LIKE 'D%';`

(iv) `mysql>SELECT Name, Section FROM STUDENT WHERE Marks BETWEEN 85 AND 100;`

31. In a database there are two tables:

Table: ITEM

Item_Code	Item_Name	Price
111	Refrigerator	90000
222	Television	75000
333	Computer	42000
444	Washing Machine	27000

Table: BRAND

Item_Code	Brand_Name
111	LG
222	Sony
333	HCL
444	IFB

Write MySQL queries for the following:

(i) To display Item_Code, Item_Name and corresponding Brand_Name of those items, whose Price is between 20000 and 40000 (both values included).

(ii) To display Item_Code, Price and Brand_Name of the item which has Item_Name as Computer.

(iii) To increase the prices of all the items by 10%.

(iv) Update the Brand_Name with Toshiba whose Item _Code is 333.

Ans. (i) `SELECT I.Item_Code, I.Item_Name,B.Brand_Name FROM ITEM I, BRAND B WHERE I.Item_Code=B.Item_Code AND I.Price BETWEEN 20000 AND 40000;`

(ii) `SELECT I.Item_Code, I.PRICE, B.Brand_Name FROM ITEM I, BRAND B Where I.Item_Code = B.Item_Code AND I.Item_Name="Computer";`

(iii) `UPDATE ITEM SET Price=Price+(Price*0.1);`

(iv) `UPDATE BRAND SET Brand_Name = 'Toshiba' WHERE Item_Code = 333;`

32. In a database Multiplexes, there are two tables with the following data. Write MySQL queries for (i) to (iv), which are based on TICKETDETAILS and AGENTDETAILS.

Table: TICKETDETAILS

Tcode	Name	Tickets	A_code
S001	Meena	7	A01
S002	Vani	5	A02
S003	Meena	9	A01
S004	Karish	2	A03
S005	Suraj	1	A02

Table: AGENTDETAILS

A_code	AName
A01	Mr. Robin
A02	Mr. Ayush
A03	Mr. Trilok
A05	Mr. Johon

(i) To display Tcode, Name and AName of all the records where the number of tickets sold is more than 5.

(ii) To display total number of tickets booked by agent "Mr. Ayush".

(iii) To display Acode, AName and corresponding Tcode where AName ends with "k".

(iv) To display maximum tickets and AName according to Acode.

Ans. (i)
```
SELECT Tcode, Name, AName
FROM TICKETDETAILS, AGENTDETAILS
WHERE TICKETDETAILS.A_code =
AGENTDETAILS.A_code AND Tickets > 5;
```
(ii)
```
SELECT AName, SUM(DISTINCT Tickets)
FROM TICKETDETAILS, AGENTDETAILS
WHERE AName = "Mr.Ayush"
AND A_Code = "A02";
```
(iii)
```
SELECT Acode, AName, Tcode
FROM TICKETDETAILS, AGENTDETAILS
WHERE TICKETDETAILS.A_code =
AGENTDETAILS.A_code AND AName LIKE
"%k";
```
(iv)
```
SELECT AName, MAX(Tickets) FROM
TICKETDETAILS,AGENTDETAILS
WHERE TICKETDETAILS.A_code
= AGENTDETAILS.A_code;
```

33. Write SQL commands for the question from (i) to (viii) on the basis of table MASTER (contains S.No. of employees)

S.No	Name	Age	Department	Salary
1	Shyam	21	Computer	12000
2	Shiv	25	Maths	15000
3	Rakesh	31	Hindi	14000
4	Sharmila	32	History	20000
5	Dushyant	25	Software	30000

(i) Write a command to update the salary of the employee to 40000, whose S. No is 3.

(ii) Write a query to add a column Date_of_ Joining to the table MASTER.

(iii) Show Age, Department of those employees whose salary is greater than 12000.

(iv) List all data of table MASTER.

(v) Write a query to change the data type of a column Name to varchar with size 35.

(vi) Write a command to delete from the table MASTER those employees whose name is Rakesh.

(vii) Write a command to update the department of the employee to english, whose name is Dushyant.

(viii) Write a command to delete the table with the structure.

Ans. (i)
```
mysql>UPDATE MASTER SET Salary= 40000
WHERE S.No =3;
```
(ii)
```
mysql>ALTER TABLE MASTER ADD
Date_of_Joining DATE;
```
(iii)
```
mysql>SELECT Age, Department FROM
MASTER WHERE Salary>12000;
```
(iv)
```
mysql>SELECT * FROM MASTER;
```
(v)
```
mysql>ALTER TABLE MASTER MODIFY Name
VARCHAR (35);
```
(vi)
```
mysql>DELETE FROM  MASTER WHERE Name =
"Rakesh";
```
(vii)
```
mysql>UPDATE MASTER SET Department =
"English" WHERE Name = "Dushyant";
```
(viii)
```
mysql>DROP TABLE MASTER;
```

34. Consider the table 'PERSONS' given below. Write commands in SQL for (i) to (iv).

Table: PERSONS

PId	SurName	FirstName	Gender	City	PinCode	BasicSalary
1	Sharma	Geet	F	Udhamwara	182141	50000
2	Singh	Surinder	M	Kupwara Nagar	193222	75000
3	Jcob	Peter	M	Bhawani	185155	45000
4	Alvis	Thomas	M	Ahmed Nagar	380025	50000
5	Mohan	Garima	M	Nagar Coolangatta	390026	33000
6	Azmi	Simi	F	New Delhi	110021	40000
7	Kaur	Manpreet	F	Udhamwara	182141	42000

(i) Display the SurName, FirstName and City of people residing in Udhamwara city.

(ii) Display the Person Id(PId), City and PinCode of PERSONS in descending order of PinCode.

(iii) Display the FirstName and City of all the females getting BasicSalary above 40000.

(iv) Display FirstName and BasicSalary of all the persons whose FirstName start with "G".

Ans (i)
```
SELECT SurName, FirstName, City FROM
PERSONS WHERE City = 'Udhamwara';
```
(ii)
```
SELECT PId, City, PinCode FROM
PERSONS   ORDER BY PinCode DESC;
```
(iii)
```
SELECT FirstName, City FROM PERSONS
WHERE Gender = 'F' AND BasicSalary >
40000;
```
(iv)
```
SELECT FirstName, BasicSalary FROM
PERSONS WHERE FirstName LIKE 'G%';
```

35. Answer the questions (i) to (iv) on the basis of the following tables SHOPPE and ACCESSORIES.

Table: SHOPPE

Id	SName	Area
S001	ABC Computeronics	CP
S002	All Infotech Media	GK II
S003	Tech Shoppe	CP
S004	Geeks Tecno Soft	Nehru Place
S005	Hitech Tech Store	Nehru Place

Table: ACCESSORIES

No	Name	Price	Id
A01	Mother Board	12000	S01
A02	Hard Disk	5000	S01
A03	Keyboard	500	S02
A04	Mouse	300	S01
A05	Mother Board	13000	S02
A06	Keyboard	400	S03
A07	LCD	6000	S04
T08	LCD	5500	S05
T09	Mouse	350	S05
T10	Hard Disk	4500	S03

(i) To display Name and Price of all the Accessories in ascending order of their Price.

(ii) To display Id and SName of all Shoppe located in Nehru Place.

(iii) To display Name, Price of all Accessories and their respective SName, where they are available.

(iv) To display name of accessories whose price is greater than 1000.

Ans. (i)
```
SELECT Name, Price
FROM ACCESSORIES
ORDER BY Price;
```
(ii)
```
SELECT Id, SName
FROM SHOPPE
WHERE Area = 'Nehru Place';
```
(iii)
```
SELECT Name, Price, SName
FROM ACCESSORIES A, SHOPPE S
WHERE A.Id = S.Id;
```
but this query enable to show the result because A.Id and S.Id are not identical.

(iv)
```
SELECT Name From
ACCESSORIES
WHERE Price>1000;
```

36. Consider the following tables STORE and answer the questions

Table : STORE

ItemNo	Item	Scode	Qty	Rate	LastBuy
2005	Sharpener Classic	23	60	8	31-JUN-09
2003	Balls	22	50	25	01-FEB-10
2002	Gel Pen Premium	21	150	12	24-FEB-10
2006	Gel Pen Classic	21	250	20	11-MAR-09
2001	Eraser Small	22	220	6	19-JAN-09
2004	Eraser Big	22	110	8	02-DEC-09
2009	Ball Pen 0.5	21	180	18	03-NOV-09

Write SQL commands for the following statements.

(i) To display details of all the items in the STORE table in ascending order of LastBuy.

(ii) To display ItemNo and Item name of those items from STORE table, whose Rate is more than ₹ 15.

(iii) To display the details of those items whose Supplier code (Scode) is 22 or Quantity in Store (Qty) is more than 110 from the table STORE.

(iv) To display the item with its quantity which include pen in their name.

Ans. (i)
```
SELECT * FROM STORE ORDER BY LastBuy;
```
(ii)
```
SELECT ItemNo, Item FROM STORE WHERE
Rate>15;
```
(iii)
```
SELECT * FROM STORE WHERE Scode = 22
OR Qty>110;
```
(iv)
```
SELECT Item, Qty FROM STORE WHERE Item
LIKE '%Pen%';
```

37. Consider the following tables STUDENT and STREAM. Write SQL commands for the statements (i) to (iv).

Table : STUDENT

SCODE	NAME	AGE	STRCDE	POINTS	GRADE
101	Amit	16	1	6	NULL
102	Arjun	13	3	4	NULL
103	Zaheer	14	2	1	NULL
105	Gagan	15	5	2	NULL
108	Kumar	13	6	8	NULL
109	Rajesh	17	5	8	NULL
110	Naveen	13	3	9	NULL
113	Ajay	16	2	3	NULL
115	Kapil	14	3	2	NULL
120	Gurdeep	15	2	6	NULL

Table: STREAM

STRCDE	STRNAME
1	SCIENCE+COMP
2	SCIENCE+BIO
3	SCIENCE+ECO
4	COMMERCE+MATHS
5	COMMERCE+SOCIO
6	ARTS+MATHS
7	ARTS+SOCIO

(i) To display the name of streams in alphabetical order from table STREAM.

(ii) To update GRADE to 'A' for all those students, who are getting more than 8 as POINTS.

(iii) ARTS+MATHS stream is no more available. Make necessary change in table STREAM.

(iv) To display student's name whose stream name is science and computer.

Ans. (i)
```
SELECT STRNAME FROM STREAM ORDER BY
STRNAME;
```
(ii)
```
UPDATE STUDENT SET GRADE = 'A' WHERE
POINTS > 8;
```
(iii)
```
DELETE FROM STREAM WHERE STRNAME
    = 'ARTS + MATHS';
```
(iv)
```
SELECT NAME FROM STUDENT WHERE
STUDENT.STRCDE = STREAM.STRCDE AND
STRNAME = "SCIENCE + COMP";
```

38. Consider the following tables GARMENT and FABRIC. Write SQL commands for the statements (i) to (iii).

Table: GARMENT

GCODE	DESCRIPTION	PRICE	FCODE	READYDATE
10023	PENCIL SKIRT	1150	F03	19-DEC-08
10001	FORMAL SHIRT	1250	F01	12-JAN-08
10012	INFORMAL SHIRT	1550	F02	06-JUN-08
10024	BABY TOP	750	F03	07-APR-07
10090	TULIP SKIRT	850	F02	31-MAR-07
10019	EVENING GOWN	850	F03	06-JUN-08
10009	INFORMAL PANT	1500	F02	20-OCT-08
10007	FORMAL PANT	1350	F01	09-MAR-08
10020	FROCK	850	F04	09-SEP-07
10089	SLACKS	750	F03	20-OCT-08

Table : FABRIC

FCODE	TYPE
F04	POLYSTER
F02	COTTON
F03	SILK
F01	TERELENE

(i) To display GCODE and DESCRIPTION of each GARMENT in descending order of GCODE.

(ii) To display the details of all the GARMENTs, which have READYDATE in between 08-DEC-07 and 16-JUN-08 (inclusive of both the dates).

(iii) To display garment's description with their price whose fabric is silk.

Ans. (i)
```
SELECT GCODE, DESCRIPTION FROM GARMENT
ORDER BY GCODE DESC;
```
(ii)
```
SELECT*FROM GARMENT WHERE READYDATE
BETWEEN '08-DEC-07' AND '16-JUN-08';
```
(iii)
```
SELECT DESCRIPTION, PRICE FROM GARMENT
WHERE GARMENT.FCODE = FABRIC.FCODE AND
TYPE = "SILK";
```

39. Consider the following tables. Write SQL commands for the statements (i) to (iv).

Table : SENDER

SenderID	SenderName	SenderAddress	SenderCity
ND01	R Jain	2, ABC Appts	New Delhi
MU02	H Sinha	12, Newtown	Mumbai
MU15	S Jha	27/A, Park Street	Mumbai
ND50	T Prasad	122-K, SDA	New Delhi

Table: RECIPIENT

RecID	SenderID	RecName	RecAddress	RecCity
KO05	ND01	R Bajpayee	5, Central Avenue	Kolkata
ND08	MU02	S Mahajan	116, A Vihar	New Delhi
MU19	ND01	H Singh	2A, Andheri East	Mumbai
MU32	MU15	P K Swamy	B5, C S Terminus	Mumbai
ND48	ND50	S Tripathi	13, B1 D, Mayur Vihar	New Delhi

(i) To display the names of all Senders from Mumbai.

(ii) To display the RecID, SenderName, SenderAddress, RecName, RecAddress for every Recipient.

(iii) To display Recipient details in ascending order of RecName.

(iv) To display the detail of recipients who are in Mumbai.

Ans. (i)
```
SELECT SenderName FROM SENDER WHERE
SenderCity = 'Mumbai';
```

(ii) SELECT RecID, SenderName,
    SenderAddress, RecName, RecAddress
    FROM RECIPIENT, SENDER WHERE
    RECIPIENT.SenderID = SENDER.SenderID;
(iii) SELECT * FROM RECIPIENT ORDER BY
    RecName;
(iv) SELECT * FROM RECIPIENT WHERE RecCity
    = "Mumbai";

40. Write the SQL commands for (i) to (v) on the basis of the table HOSPITAL.

Table: HOSPITAL

No.	Name	Age	Department	Dateofadm	Charges	Sex
1	Sandeep	65	Surgery	23/02/98	300	M
2	Ravina	24	Orthopaedic	20/01/98	200	F
3	Karan	45	Orthopaedic	19/02/98	200	M
4	Tarun	12	Surgery	01/01/98	300	M
5	Zubin	36	ENT	12/01/98	250	M
6	Ketaki	16	ENT	24/02/98	300	F
7	Ankita	29	Cardiology	20/02/98	800	F
8	Zareen	45	Gynaecology	22/02/98	300	F
9	Kush	19	Cardiology	13/01/98	800	M
10	Shailya	31	Nuclear Medicine	19/02/98	400	M

(i) To show all information about the patients of Cardiology Department.

(ii) To list the name of female patients, who are in Orthopaedic Department.

(iii) To list names of all patients with their date of admission in ascending order.

(iv) To display Patient's Name, Charges, Age for male patients only.

(v) To display name of doctor are older than 30 years and charges for consultation fee is more than 500.

Ans. (i) SELECT * FROM HOSPITAL WHERE
    Department = 'Cardiology';
(ii) SELECT Name FROM HOSPITAL WHERE
    Department = 'Orthopaedic' AND Sex
    = 'F';
(iii) SELECT Name FROM HOSPITAL ORDER BY
    Dateofadm;
(iv) SELECT Name, Charges, Age FROM
    HOSPITAL WHERE Sex = 'M';

(v) SELECT NAME FROM HOSPITAL WHERE Age>30
    AND Charges>500;

41. Write SQL commands for (i) to (v) on the basis of table INTERIORS.

Table: INTERIORS

No.	ITEMNAME	TYPE	DATEOFSTOCK	PRICE	DISCOUNT
1	Red rose	Double Bed	23/02/02	32000	15
2	Soft touch	Baby cot	20/01/02	9000	10
3	Jerry's home	Baby cot	19/02/02	8500	10
4	Rough wood	Office Table	01/01/02	20000	20
5	Comfort zone	Double Bed	12/01/02	15000	20
6	Jerry look	Baby cot	24/02/02	7000	19
7	Lion king	Office Table	20/02/02	16000	20
8	Royal tiger	Sofa	22/02/02	30000	25
9	Park sitting	Sofa	13/12/01	9000	15
10	Dine Paradise	Dining Table	19/02/02	11000	15
11	White Wood	Double Bed	23/03/03	20000	20
12	James 007	Sofa	20/02/03	15000	15
13	Tom look	Baby cot	21/02/03	7000	10

(i) To show all information about the Sofa from the INTERIORS table.

(ii) To list the ITEMNAME, which are priced at more than 10000 from the INTERIORS table.

(iii) To list ITEMNAME and TYPE of those items, in which DATEOFSTOCK is before 22/01/02 from the INTERIORS table in descending order of ITEMNAME.

(iv) To insert a new row in the INTERIORS table with the following data
    {14, 'TrueIndian', 'Office Table',
    '25/03/03', 15000, 20}

(v) To display the name of item with their price which have discount more than 20.

Ans. (i) SELECT * FROM INTERIORS WHERE TYPE
    = 'Sofa';
(ii) SELECT ITEMNAME FROM INTERIORS WHERE
    PRICE > 10000;
(iii) SELECT ITEMNAME, TYPE FROM INTERIORS
    WHERE DATEOFSTOCK < '22/01/02'
    ORDER BY ITEMNAME DESC;

(iv) ` INSERT INTO INTERIORS VALUES (14,'TrueIndian', 'Office Table',`
` '25/03/03',15000,20);`

(v) `SELECT ITEMNAM, PRICE FROM INTERIORS WHRE DISCOUNT>20;`

42. Write SQL commands for (i) to (iv) on the basis of table STUDENT.

TABLE: STUDENT

SNO	NAME	STREAM	FEES	AGE	SEX
1	ARUN KUMAR	COMPUTER	750.00	17	M
2	DIVYA JENEJA	COMPUTER	750.00	18	F
3	KESHAR MEHRA	BIOLOGY	500.00	16	M
4	HARISH SINGH	ENG. DR	350.00	18	M
5	PRACHI	ECONOMICS	300.00	19	F
6	NISHA ARORA	COMPUTER	750.00	15	F
7	DEEPAK KUMAR	ECONOMICS	300.00	16	M
8	SARIKA VASWANI	BIOLOGY	500.00	15	F

(i) List the name of all the students, who have taken stream as COMPUTER.

(ii) To display the number of students stream wise.

(iii) To display all the records in sorted order of name.

(iv) To display the stream of student whose name is Harish.

Ans. (i) `SELECT NAME FROM STUDENT WHERE STREAM ='COMPUTER';`

(ii) `SELECT STREAM, COUNT(*) FROM STUDENT GROUP BY STREAM;`

(iii) `SELECT * FROM STUDENT ORDER BY NAME;`

(iv) `SELECT STREAM FROM STUDENT WHERE NAME LIKE "%HARISH%";`

Chapter Test

Multiple Choice Questions

1. A table "Bus" exists with no rows and 6 columns . What is its cardinality?
(a) 0   (b) Such as table cannot exist
(c) 1   (d) 2

2. A table should have a
(a) foreign key   (b) alternate key
(c) primary key   (d) composite key

3. Riya wants to remove a column "Name" from her table , which command she has to use?
(a) ALTER TABLE   (b) CLEAR
(c) UPDATE   (d) None of these

4. The clause with ALTER TABLE command that renames a column is
(a) RENAME   (b) CHANGE
(c) DROP   (d) CHANGENAME

5. A table can have .... alternate keys.
(a) 1   (b) 2
(c) 3   (d) multiple

Short Answer Type Questions

6. Explain the use of alias in a query statement.

7. Explain usage of IS NULL and IS NOT NULL clauses.   **(NCERT)**

8. With respect to the following table structure write queries for the following

GameID	GName	Type	Players

(i) To display the details of games of "OUTDOOR" type.
(ii) To display GName and Players for games where players is more than 2.

9. Explain working of AND and OR operators in queries.

10. An organization ABC maintains a database EMP_DEPENDENT to record the following details about its employees and their dependents.   **(NCERT)**

EMPLOYEE(AadhaarNo, Name, Address, Department, EmpID)

DEPENDENT(EmpID, DependentName, Relationship)

Use the EMP_DEPENDENT database to answer the following SQL queries:

(i) Find employee details working in a department, say 'PRODUCTION'.
(ii) Find employee names having no dependent.

Long Answer Type Questions

11. With respect to the following table "BOOK" write SQL queries

Table : Book

BookID	Bname	Publisher	Price	DtofPub
B1	Science Fiction	TMH	1200	2020-09-08
B2	Stories	PHI	900	NULL
B3	Ramayana	PHI	1700	NULL
B4	Beginners Cooking	Oswal	1400	1990-12-03

(i) Display details of books published before year 2000.
(ii) Display names and publishers of books whose price is less than 1000.
(iii) Display names of books who do not have a date of publication.
(iv) Increase price of all books by 200.

12. Write SQL queries with respect to the Employee table given below.

Table : Employee

Eno	Ename	Dept	Desig	DtofJoin	Salary
1	Jack	Sales	MGR	2012-09-12	89000
2	Priya	Accts	MGR	2005-04-22	56000
3	Ria	Pers	Clerk	2000-01-09	25000
4	Anil	Pers	Officer	1994-04-03	67000
5	Sumit	Sales	Officer	NULL	19000
6	Akash	Sales	Officer	NULL	20000

(i) Display name and department of employees whose name begins with" S".

(ii) Display details of employees whose designation ends with "r".

(iii) Display details of employees whose name has 1st letter "P" 3rd letter "i".

(iv) Display name,deptartment and salary of employees whose department name ends with "s".

13. Given the two tables.

Table : Student

Roll	Name	Marks	Hostelld
1	Fiza	89	H1
2	Swati	78	H2
3	Anil	55	H3
4	Ria	68	H4
5	Prakash	12	H5

Table : Hostel

Hostelld	Hname	Location
H1	Ganga	Kol
H2	Yamuna	Che
H3	Satluj	Mum
H4	Godavari	Bang

(i) Identify the primary keys of the two tables.

(ii) Identify the foreign key of Student table.

(iii) Can a student have HostelID "H5"?

Answers

Multiple Choice Questions

1. (b) *2. (c)* *3. (a)* *4. (b)* *5. (d)*

For Detailed Solutions

Scan the code

Emerging Trends

In this Chapter...

- Artificial Intelligence (AI)
- Big Data
- Internet of Things (IoT)
- Cloud Computing
- Grid Computing
- Blockchain Technology

Computers have been around for quite some time now. New technologies and initiatives emerge with each passing day. In order to understand the existing technologies and have a better view of the development around us, we must keep an eye on the emerging trends.

Many new technologies are introduced almost every day. Some of these do not succeed and fade away over time. Some of these new technologies prosper and persist over time, gaining attention from users.

Emerging trends are the state of the art technologies, which gain popularity and set a new trend among users. In this chapter, we will learn about some emerging trends that will make a huge impact on digital economy and interaction in digital societies.

Artificial Intelligence (AI)

Artificial Intelligence (AI) is an area of computer science that emphasises the creation of intelligent machines that work and react like humans.

The term may also be applied to any machine that exhibits traits associated with a human mind such as learning and problem-solving.

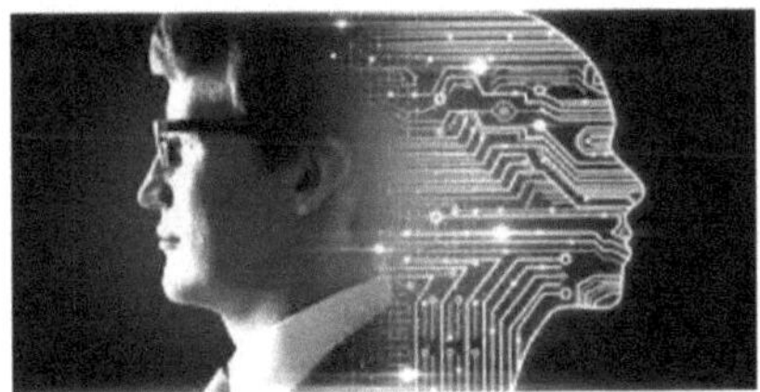

Knowledge engineering is a core part of AI research. Machines can often act and react like humans only if they have abundant information relating to the world.

Artificial intelligence must have access to objects, categories, properties and relations between all of them to implement knowledge engineering.

Types of Artificial Intelligence

Artificial intelligence can be categorised into two parts, which are as follows

(i) **Weak AI** It embodies a system designed to carry out one particular job. Weak AI systems include video games and personal assistants such as the chess and Amazon's Alexa, respectively.

(ii) **Strong AI** These systems are systems that carry on the tasks considered to be human like. Strong AI tend to be more complex and complicated systems. These kinds of systems can be found in applications like self-driving cars, in hospital operating rooms etc.

Applications of Artificial Intelligence

There are some applications of artificial intelligence, which are as follows

(i) **In Banking** A lot of banks have already adopted AI-based systems to provide customer support, detect anomalies and credit card frauds. AI solutions can be used to enhance security across a number of business sector, including retail and finance.

(ii) **In Gaming** Over the past few years, AI has become an integral part of the gaming industry. In fact, one of the biggest accomplishment of AI is in the gaming industry.

(iii) **In Healthcare** Companies are applying machine learning to make better and faster diagnoses than humans. One of the best known technologies is IBM's Watson. It understands natural language and can respond to questions asked it.

(iv) **In Business** Robotic process automation is being applied to highly repetitive tasks normally performed by humans. Machine learning algorithms are being integrated into analytics and CRM (Customer Relationship Management) platforms to uncover information on how to better serve customers.

(v) **In Autonomous Vehicles** Just like humans, self driving cars need to have sensors to understand the world around them and a brain to collect, processes and choose specific actions based on information gathered. Autonomous vehicles are with advanced tool to gather information, including long range radar, cameras and LIDAR (Light Detection and Ranging).

(vi) **In Social Media** In social media platforms like facebook, AI is used for face verification wherein machine learning and deep learning concepts are used to detect facial features and tag your friends.

Machine Learning

Machine learning is a sub-system of artificial intelligence, wherein computers have the ability to learn from data using statistical techniques, without being explicitly programmed by a human being.

It comprises algorithms that use data to learn on their own and make predictions. These algorithms, called models, are first trained and tested using a training data and testing data, respectively. After successive trainings, once these models are able to give results to an acceptable level of accuracy, they are used to make predictions about new and unknown data.

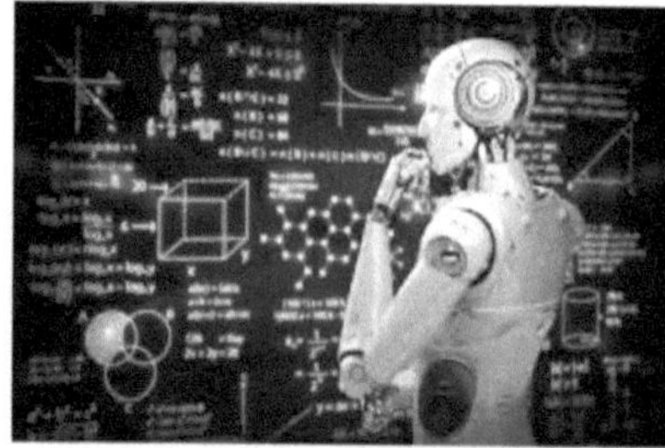

Machine learning is an important component of the growing field of data science. Through the use of statistical methods, algorithms are trained to make classifications or predictions, uncovering key insights within data mining projects. These insights subsequently drive decision making within

applications and businesses, ideally impacting key growth metrics. As big data continues to expand and grow, the market demand for data scientists will increase, requiring them to assist in the identification of the most relevant business questions and subsequently the data to answer them.

Natural Language Processing (NLP)

The predictive typing feature of search engines that helps us by suggesting the next word in the sentence while typing keywords and the spell checking features are examples of Natural Language Processing (NLP). It deals with the interaction between human and computers using human spoken languages, such as Hindi, English, etc.

In fact, it is possible to search the web or operate or control our devices using our voice. All this has been possible by NLP. An NLP system can perform text-to-speech and speech-to-text conversion.

Some applications of Natural Language Processing are

- Sentiment Analysis
- Text Classification
- Chatbots & Virtual Assistants
- Text Extraction
- Machine Translation
- Text Summarization
- Market Intelligence
- Auto-Correct
- Intent Classificaion
- Urgency Detection
- Speech Recognition

Immersive Experiences

With the three dimensional (3D) videography, the joy of watching movies in theaters have reached to a new level video games are also being developed to provide immersive experiences to the player. Immersive experiences allow us to visualise, feel and react by stimulating over senses. It enhances our interaction and involvement, making them more realistic and engaging.

Immersive experiences have been used in the field of training, such as driving simulators, flight simulator and so on. Immersive experiences can be achieved using virtual reality and augmented reality.

1. Virtual Reality

Virtual Reality (VR) is the use of computer technology to create a simulated environment. Unlike traditional user interfaces, VR places the user inside an experience. Instead of viewing a screen in front of them, users are immersed and able to interact with 3D worlds.

Virtual reality is an artificial environment that is created with software and presented to the user in such a way that the user suspends belief and accepts it as a real environment. On a computer, virtual reality is primarily experienced through two of the five senses: Sight and Sound.

There are several applications of virtual reality technology in human lives, some of them are discussed below

(i) **In Gaming** Virtual technology's devices are used for virtual gaming experiences. Along with this, devices such as Wi-Fi Remote, PlayStation Move/Eye, Kinect are based on virtual reality which track and send input of the players to the game.

(ii) **In Healthcare** Healthcare is one of the applications where virtual reality could have the most significant impact. Health care professionals can now use virtual models to prepare them for working on a real body. Virtual reality can also be used as a treatment for mental health issues.

(iii) **In Education** Virtual reality has been adopted in education too. It improves teaching and learning. With virtual reality, a large group of students can interact with one another within a three-dimensional environment.

(iv) **In Engineering and Architecture** Virtual reality plays a major role in simulating three-dimensional models infrastructures, designs which can provide a real-life experience of the physical designs or infrastructures before hand. This helps in reducing considerable costs and expenses which can be incurred in a prototype.

(v) **In Entertainment** Virtual reality is being used in the entertainment industry to boost experiences with 360 films and increase emotional connection with them and/or the characters.

(vi) **In Business** Virtual reality has also been adopted in business. It is now being used for virtual tours of a business environment, training of new employees and this also gives new employees a 360 degree view of every product.

2. Augmented Reality

Augmented reality (AR) is an enhanced version of the real physical world that is achieved through the use of digital visual elements, sound or other sensory stimuli delivered *via* technology. It is a growing trend among companies involved in mobile computing and business applications in particular.

Augmented reality is a technology that extends the user's view of the real world with digital, virtual content. AR enhances, extends or teaches about the real world with in-context digital content.

The superimposition of computer generated perceptual information over the existing physical surroundings is called as Augmented Reality (AR). It adds components of the digital world to the physical world, along with the associated tactile and other sensory requirements, thereby making the environment interactive and digitally manipulable.

There are few applications of augmented reality, which are as follows

(i) **In Surgery** Augmented reality and the healthcare industry seem like the perfect match. Complicated medical procedures could be massively improved using AR technology surgery can be risky and even seasoned surgeons can make mistakes.

(ii) **In Engineering** Production and manufacturing have been disrupted by innovative technology. Augmented Reality has provided another tool for the creation and maintenance of complicated and expensive machines, making it easier for engineers to carry out repairs.

(iii) **In Military** Despite seeming like a relatively new application of Augmented reality, the first fully functioning. AR system was developed at the US Air Force Research Laboratory back in 1992.

Robotics

A robot is basically a machine capable of carrying out one or more tasks automatically with accuracy and precision. Unlike other machines, a robot is programmable, which means it can follow the instructions given through computer programs. Robots were initially conceptualised for doing repetitive industrial tasks that are boring or stressful for humans or were labour intensive.

Sensors are one of the prime components of a robot. Robot can be of many types, such as wheeled robots, legged robots, manipulators and humanoids. Robots that resemble humans are known as humanoids. Robots are being used in industries medical science, bionics, scientific research, military etc. Some examples are

- NASA's Mars Exploration Rover (MER) mission is a robotic space mission to study about a planet mars.

- Sophia is a humanoid that uses artificial intelligence, visual data processing, facial recognition and also imitates human gestures and facial expressions.

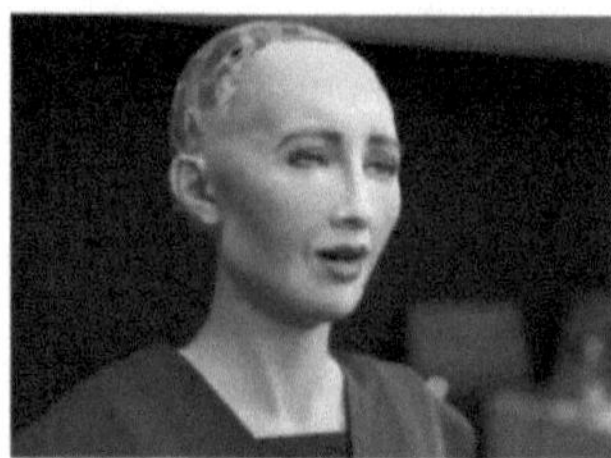

- A drone is an unmanned aircraft which can be remotely controlled or can fly autonomously through software controlled flight plans in their embedded systems. Drones are being used in many fields, such as journalism, filming and aerial photography, shipping or delivery at short distances, disaster management, search and rescue operations, healthcare, geographic mapping and structural safety inspections, agriculture, wildlife monitoring, besides law enforcement.

Generally, there are five types of robots

- Pre-programmed robots
- Humanoid robots
- Autonomous robots
- Tele-operated robots
- Augmenting robots

Advantages of Robots in the Workplace

The advantages of robots in the workplace are

- **Safety** Safety is the most obvious advantage of utilising robotics.
- **Speed** Robots don't get distracted or need to take breaks.
- **Consistency** Robots never need to divide their attention between a multitude of things.
- **Perfection** Being machines working on data , they produce perfect results.
- **Happier Employees** As these robots learn more about their environments and perform simple, repetitive tasks without the need for intervention, humans can focus on higher-level tasks, which leads to improved rates of employee satisfaction.

- **Job creation** When some of the rote elements of a job are eliminated, the higher-skilled parts of the job become more important. With automation, there will be a large net increase in jobs.
- **Productivity** Since they are electromechanical devices they work at faster rate than human beings and can work for longer durations.

Disadvantages of Robots in the Workplace

The disadvantages of robots in the workplace are

- They lead humans to lose their Jobs.
- They need constant power.
- They are restricted to their programming.
- They perform relatively few tasks.
- They have no emotions.
- They impact human interaction.
- They require expertise to set them up.

Big Data

The definition of big data is data that contains greater variety, arriving in increasing volumes and with more velocity.Put simply, big data is larger, more complex data sets, especially from new data sources. These data sets are so voluminous that traditional data processing software just cannot manage them.

Extremely large data sets that may be analysed computationally to reveal patterns, trends, and associations, especially relating to human behaviour and interactions.

Big data is the set of technologies created to store, analyse and manage this bulk data, a macro-tool created to identify patterns in the chaos of this explosion in information in order to design smart solutions. Today it is used in areas as diverse as medicine, agriculture, gambling and environmental protection.

Characterisitics of Big Data

Some characteristics of big data are as follows

(i) **Variety** Variety of big data refers to structured, unstructured and semi-structured data, i.e. gathered from multiple sources.

While in the past, data could only be collected from spreadsheets and databases, today data comes in an array of forms such as E-mails, PDFs, Photos, etc.

(ii) **Velocity** It essentially refers to the speed at which data is being created in real-time. In a broader prospect, it comprises the rate of change and linking of incoming data sets at varying speeds.

(iii) **Volume** Big data indicates huge volumes of data that is being generated on a daily basis from various sources like social media platforms, business processes, machines, networks, etc.

Applications of Big Data

There are some applications of big data are as follows

(i) **In Government** When government agencies are harnessing and applying analytics to their big data, they have improvised a lot in terms of managing utilities, running agencies, dealing with traffic congestion or preventing the crimes.

(ii) **In Healthcare** Big data had already started to create a huge difference in the healthcare sector.

With the help of predictive analytics, medical professionals can now able to provide personalised healthcare services to individual patient.

(iii) **In Banking** The banking sector relies on big data for fraud detection. Big data tools can efficiently detect fraudulent acts in real time such as misuse of credit/debit cards etc.

(iv) **In Manufacturing** Using big data manufacturing industry can improve product quality and output while minimizing waste.

Big Data Analytics

The term data analytics refers to the process of examining datasets to draw conclusions about the information they contain. Data analytic techniques enable you to take raw data and uncover patterns to extract valuable insights from it.

Data analytics is vital in analysing surveys, polls, public opinion, etc. *For example*, It helps segment audiences by different demographic groups and analyse attitudes and trends in each of them, producing more specific, accurate and actionable snapshots of public opinion.

There are four types of analytics, Descriptive, Diagnostic, Predictive and Prescriptive.

Internet of Things (IoT)

Internet of Things (IoT) is a network of physical objects or people called "things" that are embedded with software, electronics, network and sensors that allows these objects to collect and exchange data. The thing in IoT can also be a person with a diabetes monitor implant, an animal with tracking devices, etc.

The Internet of Things (IoT) refers to a system of interrelated, internet-connected objects that are able to collect and transfer data over a wireless network without human intervention. The personal or business possibilities are endless. Businesses also are driven by a need for regulatory compliance.

In short, the Internet of Things (IoT) refers to the rapidly growing network of connected objects that are able to collect and exchange data in real time using embedded sensors. Cars, lights, refrigerators and more appliances can all be connected to the IoT.

For example, If a microwave oven, an air conditioner, door lock, CCTV camera or other such devices are enabled to connect to the Internet, we can access and remotely control them on-the-go using our smartphone.

Components of IoT

There are four fundamental components of IoT system, which are as follows

(i) **Sensors/Devices** These are key components that help you to collect live data from the surrounding environment. All this data may have various levels of complexities. It could be a simple temperature monitoring sensor or it may be in the form of the video feed. The display also changes to vertical or horizontal with respect to the way we hold our mobile. This is possible with the help of two sensors, namely accelerometer and gyroscope. The accelerometer sensor in the mobile phones detects the orientation of the phone. The gyroscope sensors track rotation or twist of your hand and add to the information supplied by the accelerometer.

(ii) **Connectivity** All the collected data is sent to a cloud infrastructure. The sensors should be connected to the cloud using various media of communication. These communication media include Mobile or Satellite networks, Bluetooth, Wi-Fi, WAN, etc.

(iii) **Data Processing** Once the data is collected and it gets to the cloud, the software performs processing on the gathered data. This process can be just checking the temperature, reading on devices like AC or heaters. However, it can sometimes also be very complex like identifying objects using computer vision on video.

(iv) **User Interface** The information made available to the end user in some ways. This can achieve by triggering alarms on their phones or notifying through text or E-mails. Also, a user sometimes might also have an interface through which they can actively check in on their IoT system.

Advantages of IoT

There are following advantages of IoT as follows

(i) **Technical Optimisation** IoT technology helps a lot in improving technologies and making them better.

(ii) **Reduce Waste** IoT offers real time information leading to effective decision-making and management of resources.

(iii) **Improved Customer Engagement** IoT allows you to improve customer experience by detecting problems and improving the process.

(iv) **Improved Data Collection** Traditional data collection has its limitations and its design for passive use.

Disadvantages of IoT

There are following disadvantages of IoT as follows

(i) **Security** As the IoT systems are interconnected and communicate over networks, the system offers little control despite any security measures. It can lead the various kinds of network attacks.

(ii) **Privacy** Even without the active participation of the user, IoT system provides substantial personal data in maximum detail.

(iii) **Complexity** The designing, developing, maintaining and enabling the large technology to IoT system is quite complicated.

Web of Things (WoT)

The Web of Things (WoT) is a computing concept that describes a future where everyday objects are fully integrated with the Web. Such smart devices would then be able to communicate with each other using existing web standards.

While IoT is about creating a network of objects, things, people, systems and applications, WoT tries to integrate them to the Web.However, the scope of IoT applications is broader and includes systems that are not accessible through the web.

The Web of Things (WoT) seeks to counter the fragmentation of the IoT by using and extending existing, standardised web technologies. By providing standardized metadata and other re-usable technological building blocks, W3C WoT enables easy integration across IoT platforms and application domains.

Smart City

A smart city uses Information and Communication Technology (ICT) to improve operational efficiency, share information with the public and provide a better quality of government service and citizen welfare. People are able to live and work within the city, using its resources.

In general, a smart city is a city that uses technology to provide services and solve city problems. A smart city does things like improve transportation and accessibility, improve social services, promote sustainability, and give its citizens a voice.

How Does a Smart City Work?

A smart city collects and analyses data from IoT sensors and video cameras. In essence, it senses the environment so that the city operator can decide how and when to take action. Some actions can be performed automatically.
For example, a public waste bin can contact the city for service when it is near capacity instead of waiting for a scheduled pickup.

Benefits of a Smart City

(i) **For City Agencies** Gain more citizen engagement and optimize operations through real-time data intelligence and intra-agency collaboration.

(ii) **For Citizens** Improve daily life through city service. Smart cities offer visibility into real time city data for improving mobility, connectivity and safety services.

(iii) **For Businesses** Drive new revenue stream and economic development by enhancing awareness of customer activity and behavior.

(iv) **For Development and Vendors** Fuel application development of city data. Help the city improve operational efficiences, engage citizens and boost economic viability.

Disadvantages of Smart City

- Lack of public awareness and social responsibility.
- Building and maintaining the infrastructure is costly and challenging.
- Demands 24×7 connectivity and power supply.
- Security issues in terms of public data.
- May lead a way towards social discrimination.

Cloud Computing

In the simplest terms, cloud computing means storing and accessing data and programs over the internet instead of your computer's hard drive. When you store data or run programs from the hard drive, that's called local storage and computing.

Cloud computing refers to remote access of hardware/software resources for access, configuration, manipulation. Cloud computing offers online data storage, infrastructure, and application. Applications such as Customer Relationship Management (CRM), E-mail, web conferencing, execute on cloud.

Characteristics of Cloud Computing

The characteristics of cloud computing are as follows

(i) **On Demand Self Services** Computer services such as E-mail, applications, network or server service can be provided without requiring human interaction with each service provider.

(ii) **Broad Network Access Cloud** capabilities are available over the network and accessed through standard mechanisms that promote use by heterogeneous thin or thick client platforms such as mobile phones, laptops, PDAs, etc.

(iii) **Resource Pooling** The provider's computing resources are pooled together to serve multiple consumers using multiple-tenant model with different physical and virtual resources dynamically assigned and reassigned according to consumer demand.

(iv) **Rapid Elasticity** Cloud services can be rapidly and elastically provisioned, in some cases automatically, to quickly scale IN/OUT and rapidly released to quickly scale in.

(v) **Measured Service** Cloud computing resource usage can be measured, controlled and reported providing transparency for both the provider and consumer of the utilized service.

(vi) **Multi Tenacity** It refers to the need for policy-driven enforcement, segmentation, isolation, governance, service levels and chargeback/billing models for different consumer constituencies.

Types of Cloud Deployments

There are three types of cloud deployments categorized based on an organization's ability to manage and secure assets as follows

(i) **Public Cloud** It is managed by third party which provides cloud services over the Internet to public. They offer solutions for minimizing IT infrastructure costs and act as a good option for handling peak loads on the local infrastructure. A public cloud is meant to serve multiple users, not a single customer.

(ii) **Private Cloud** It is distributed system that works on a private infrastructure and providing the users with dynamic provisioning of computing resources.

(iii) **Hybrid Cloud** It is a heterogeneous distributed system resulted by combining facilities of public cloud and private cloud. For this reason, they are also called heterogeneous clouds.

Cloud Computing Services

The Most common and widely used cloud computing services are

(i) **Infrastructure as a Service (IaaS)** It is a cloud computing model where virtualized infrastructure is offered to and managed for business by external cloud providers. Some examples of the wide usage of IaaS are automated, policy-driven operations such as backup, recovery, etc.

(ii) **Software as a Service (SaaS)** It is a method for delivering software applications over the Internet as per the demand and on a subscription basis. Most common examples of SaaS are MicrosoftOffice 360, Oracle CRM, Marketo, etc.

(iii) **Platform as a Service (PaaS)** It refers to the supply on-demand environment for developing, testing, delivering and managing software applications. Some key players offering PaaS are Bluemix, CloudBees, Salesforce.com, etc.

Applications of Cloud Computing

The applications of cloud computing are limitless. With the right middleware, a cloud computing system could execute all the programs a normal computer could run. Potentially, everything from generic word processing software to customized computer programs designed for a specific company could work on a cloud computing system.

There are some applications of cloud computing, which are as follows

(i) Clients would be able to access their applications and data from anywhere at any time.

(ii) It could bring hardware costs down. You would not need a large hard drive because you'd store all your information on a remote computer.

(iii) Corporations that rely on computers have to make sure they have the right software in place to achieve goals. Cloud computing systems give these organisations company-wide access to computer applications. The companies do not have to buy a set of softwares or software licenses for every employee. Instead, the company could pay a metered fee to a cloud computing company.

(iv) Servers and digital storage devices take up space. Some companies rent physical space to store servers and databases because they do not have it available on site. Cloud computing gives these companies the option for storing data on someone else's hardware, removing the need for physical space on the front end.

(v) Corporations might save money on IT support. Streamlined hardware would, in theory, have fewer problems than a network of heterogeneous machines and operating systems.

Grid Computing

Grid computing is a distributed computing architecture. In grid computing, resources are used in collaborative pattern and users need do not to pay for use. Grid computing is a group of networked computers which work together as a virtual supercomputer to perform large tasks, such as analysing huge sets of data or weather modeling.

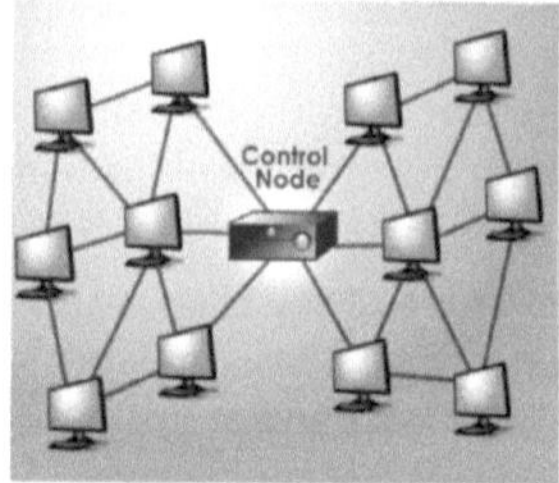

Unlike with parallel computing, grid computing projects typically have no time dependency associated with them.

For example, a corporation that allocates a set of computer nodes running in a cluster to jointly perform a given task is a simple example of grid computing in action.

There are three types of grid compating, which are as follows

(i) **Computational Grid** It acts as the resource of many computers in a network to a single problem at a time.

(ii) **Data Grid** It deals with the controlled sharing and management of distributed data of large amount.

(iii) **Collaborative Grid** It is the grid which solves collaborative problems.

Grid computing enables the virtualisation of distributed computing resources such as processing, network bandwidth, and storage capacity to create a single system image, granting users and applications seamless access to vast IT capabilities.

Blockchains Technology

Blockchain technology is most simply defined as a decentralised, distributed ledger that records the provenance of a digital asset.

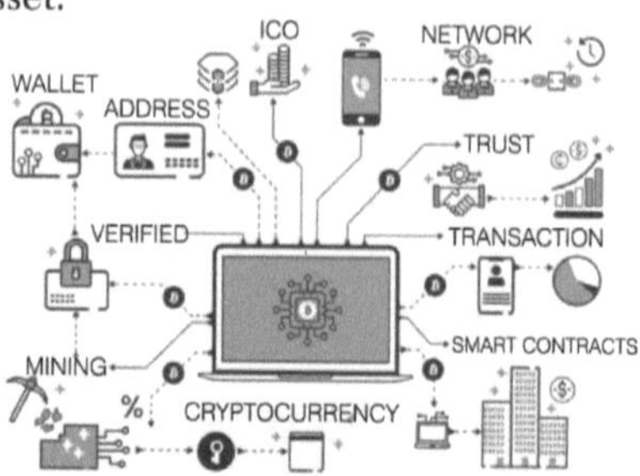

Blockchain is a system of recording information in a way that makes it difficult or impossible to change, hack or cheat the system. A blockchain is essentially a digital ledger of transactions that is duplicated and distributed across the entire network of computer systems on the blockchain.

Blockchain technology can be used to create a permanent, public, transparent ledger system for compiling data on sales, tracking digital use and payments to content creators, such as wireless users or musicians.

It is a chain of blocks which contain information.

How Blockchains Work?

When a new transaction or an edit to an existing transaction comes into a blockchain, generally a majority of the nodes within a blockchain implementation must execute algorithms to evaluate and verify the history of the individual blockchain block that is proposed.

If a majority of the nodes come to a consensus that the history and signature is valid, the new block of transactions is accepted into the ledger and a new block is added to the chain of transactions. If a majority does not concede to the addition or modification of the ledger entry, it is denied and not added to the chain.

This distributed consensus model is what allows blockchain to run as a distributed ledger without the need for some central, unifying authority saying that transactions are valid and which ones are not.

Advantages of Blockchain Technology

(i) It allows smart devices to speak to each other better and faster.

(ii) It allows the removal of intermediaries that are involved in record keeping and transfer of assets.

(iii) It provides durability, reliability and longevity with decentralized network.

(iv) The data that are entered in blockchain based systems are immutable which prevents against fraud through manipulating transactions and the history of data.

(v) It brings everyone to the highest degree of accountability.

Chapter Practice

Objective Questions

• Multiple Choice Questions

1. Which of the following is not a emerging trend in technology?

(a) Sensors   (b) Smart cities

(c) Blockchains   (d) Fax machines

Ans. (d) Fax machines is not a recent technology and has been in use for quite a long time for sending documents using telephone network.

2. Which of the following is not a service in cloud computing?

(a) IaaS   (b) SaaS

(c) PaaS   (d) NaaS

Ans. (d) IaaS, SaaS , PaaS are all services available in cloud computing .

3. Which of the following is/are type(s) of grid computing?

(a) Data grid   (b) Collaborative grid

(c) Both (a) and (b)   (d) None of these

Ans. (c) There are three types of grid computing as

(i) Data grid

(ii) Collaborative grid

(iii) Computational grid

4. IaaS stands for

(a) Indian Administration Service

(b) Intenet as a Service

(c) Infrastructure as a Service

(d) Information as a Service

Ans. (c) IaaS stands for Infrastructure as a Service, a type of service in cloud computing.

5. Which of the following function(s) is/are possible by a robot?

(a) Helping in daily activities

(b) Helping in computation

(c) Helping in industries

(d) All of the above

Ans. (d) All the functions listed in the options are possible by the robots.

6. NLP stands for

(a) Natural Language Processing

(b) New Language Processing

(c) New Logical Program

(d) Natural Looking Program

Ans. (a) It is the ability of a computer program to understand human language as it is spoken and written -referred to as natural language. It is a component of artificial intelligence.

7. In grid computing, a grid is

(a) a modem

(b) a router

(c) any network device

(d) a computer

Ans. (d) Grid computing is a group of network computers which work together as a virtual super computer to perform large tasks.

8. Which of the following is/are an advantage(s) of blockchain technology?

(a) It allows smart devices to speak to each other better and faste.

(b) It provides durability.

(c) It provides reliability.

(d) All of the above

Ans. (d) The blockchain technology provides durability, reliability and longevity with decentralised network and it allows smart devices to speak to each other better and faster.

9. AR stands for

(a) All Reality

(b) Artificial Reality

(c) Augmented Reality

(d) Artistic Reality

Ans. (c) AR is a sub-version of immersive experiences, standing for Augmented Reality.

10. Mohan found that he could search for a product in a shopping site using voice search. This is an instance of

(a) Natural language processing

(b) Immersive experience

(c) Grid computing

(d) Block chain technology

Ans. (a) Predictive typing , speech recognition etc., are all applications of natural language processing , that help human beings make their searching process comfortable and faster.

11. .... uses a system of distributed computing to process large tasks using multiple nodes in a network.

(a) Grid computing   (b) Cloud computing

(c) Block chain technology   (d) None of these

Ans. (*a*) Grid computing is a group of networked computers which work together as a virtual supercomputer to perform large tasks, such as analysing huge sets of data or weather modeling.

12. Which of the following is not a characteristic of Big Data?

(a) Volume   (b) Velocity

(c) Variety   (d) Variable

Ans. (*d*) The five characteristics of big data are : Volume, Velocity, Variety ,Veracity and Value. The term Big Data refers to all the data that accumulates from different data sources. This data is not only of enormous volume but also grows rapidly, is of large varieties and contains data of rich value.

13. Which among the following makes transactions more safer?

(a) Grid computing

(b) Block Chains

(c) Virtual reality

(d) Augmented reality

Ans. (*b*) Blockchain technology is most simply defined as a decentralized, distributed ledger that records the provenance of a digital asset. By inherent design, the data on a blockchain is unable to be modified, which makes it a legitimate disruptor for industries like payments, cybersecurity and healthcare.

14. Mohini found that while looking at a thriller movie the environment around her was changing , giving her a feel of as if she was in the Movie. This is done using

(a) Natural Language Processing

(b) Immersive Experience

(c) Robotics

(d) None of the above

Ans. (*b*) An immersive experience pulls a person into a new or augmented reality, enhancing everyday life (by making it more engaging or satisfying) via technology. They often use one or more technologies linked together.

15. The different types of GRIDS in Grid computing are

(a) Data Grid

(b) Computational Grid

(c) Collaborative Grid

(d) All of the aboave

Ans. (*d*) Grid Computing can be defined as a network of computers working together to perform a task that would rather be difficult for a single machine. Types of Grid computing are : Data Grid,Computational Grid and Collaborative Grid.

• Case Based MCQs

Direction *Read the case and answer the following questions.*

16. Mr. Jack as Mechanical Engineer is not very conversant with the emerging technologies of today. He wants to be clear about some of the terms that he gets to hear here and there everyday . Help him with the correct options to be clear about the terms.

(i) A kind of technology, where human like machines are built with injected technology to help people in different tasks .

(a) Cloud computing   (b) VoIP

(c) Blockchains   (d) Robotics

(ii) He heard that some cities are smart, what is meant by a smart city?

(a) A city with smart people

(b) A city with smart cars

(c) A city built with smart infrastructure that can communicate to a central controlling location

(d) A city with robots

(iii) He found that when he types anything in Google search , the suggestions arrive in the list .This is an instance of

(a) robotics

(b) blockchain technology

(c) natural language processing

(d) All of the above

(iv) He found a new movie in the town that gives feelings and puts the audience in the situation of the movie. This is an instance of

(a) immersive experience   (b) robotic technology

(c) NLP   (d) None of these

(v) He wanted to know that which senses are used in virtual reality?

(a) Sight and Touch   (b) Sight and Sound

(c) Sight and Smell   (d) None of these

Ans. (i) (*d*) Robotics is an emerging technology, where human resembling machines are built with embedded knowledge and intelligence to perform and assist in human activities.

(ii) (*c*) In general, a smart city is a city that uses technology to provide services and solve city problems.

(iii) (*c*) Autolist of suggestions appearing in Google search is an instance of natural language processing.

(iv) (*a*) An immersive experience is one that pulls a person into a new or augmented reality.

(v) (*b*) Virtual reality is primarily experienced through two of the five senses Sight and Sound.

A smart city uses Information and Communication Technology (ICT) to improve operational efficiency, share information with the public and provide a better quality of government service and citizen welfare. People are able to live and work within the city, using its resources.

17. Ms. Paramita a Research Scholar at Calcutta University has got a new project on Robot development. She is not very conversant about robots and robotics. Help her by solving the questions regarding robots to make her concepts clear.

(i) Which of the following is not true about robots?
(a) They have life
(b) They work on artificial intelligence
(c) They can have visual features also
(d) Both (b) and (c)

(ii) Which of the following is/are type(s) of robots?
(a) Humanoids   (b) Pre-programmed
(c) Tele-operated   (d) All of these

(iii) Which of the following branch is not a part of robotics?
(a) Computer engineering   (b) Mechanical engineering
(c) Electrical engineering   (d) Chemical engineering

(iv) Which of the following statement(s) concerning the implementation of robotic systems is/are correct?
(a) Implementation of robots can save existing jobs.
(b) Implementation of robots can create new jobs.
(c) Robotics could prevent a business from closing.
(d) All of the above

(v) A robot is
(a) programmable   (b) non-programmable
(c) Both (a) and (b)   (d) None of these

Ans. (i) (*a*) Robots are devices engineered by human beings . They do no have life.
(ii) (*d*) Robots can be Humanoids look like humans , Pre-programmed or Tele-operated by telephone.
(iii) (*d*) Robot development is based on Computer, Mechanical and Electrical engineering principles.
(iv) (*d*) Robotics can save existing jobs , create jobs and help businesses to develop from adverse situations.
(v) (*a*) Since robots are human designed, comprising of intelligence , electronic boards and programs , they are programmable.

PART 2
Subjective Questions

• Short Answer Type Questions

1. List some of the cloud-based services that you are using at present.   **(NCERT)**

Ans. (i) **IaaS** cloud-based services, pay-as-you-go for services such as storage, networking and virtualisation.
(ii) **PaaS** hardware and software tools available over the Internet.
(iii) **SaaS** software that's available *via* a third-party over the Internet.

2. Write full forms of the following
(i) VR   (ii) AR   (iii) AI   (iv) IoT

Ans. (i) VR – Virtual Reality
(ii) AR – Augmented Reality
(iii) AI – Artificial Intelligence
(iv) IoT – Internet of Things

3. Write a short note on NLP.

Ans. NLP stands for Natural Language Processing . It is one of the emerging trends. In natural language processing, human language is separated into fragments so that the grammatical structure of sentences and the meaning of words can be analysed and understood in context. This helps computers read and understand spoken or written text in the same way as humans.

4. What do you understand by IoT? Write some of its applications.   **(NCERT)**

Ans. Internet of Things (IoT) is a phenomenon that connects the things (the smart devices) to the internet over wired or wireless connections.

Some of its potential applications are as follows
(i) **Home appliance** Some examples of home appliances are fridges, cookers, coffee makers, heaters, HVAC, TVs, DVD players, lights, doors, windows etc.
(ii) **Wearables** Some examples of wearbles are clothes, shoes, hats, watches, heart monitors etc.
(iii) **Vehicles** Some examples of vehicles are cars, buses, bicycles, trains etc.
(iv) **Factories** Some examples of factories are machines, robots, warehouse shelves, parts within machines, tools etc.
(v) **Agriculture** Bio-chip transponders on farm animals and plants, farm humidity and temperature sensors etc.
(vi) **Food** Sensors for monitoring the condition of food.

5. Write a short note on cloud computing.   **(NCERT)**

Ans. Cloud computing is internet-based computing, whereby shared resources, software and information are provided to computers and other devices on demand, like the electricity grid.

A basic definition of cloud computing is the use of the Internet for the tasks you perform on your computer for storage, retrieval and access. The "cloud" represents the Internet. Cloud computing services are delivered through a network, usually the Internet.

6. What are sensors used for? Write its types.

Ans. People use sensors to measure temperature, gauge distance, detect smoke, regulate pressure and a myriad of other uses. Because analog signals are continuous, they can account for the slightest change in the physical variable (such as temperature or pressure).

The most frequently used different types of sensors are classified based on the quantities such as Electric current or Potential or Magnetic or Radio sensors, Humidity sensor, Fluid velocity or Flow sensors, Pressure sensors, Thermal or Heat or Temperature sensors, Proximity sensors, Optical sensors.

7. What is on-demand service? How it is provided in cloud computing? **(NCERT)**

Ans. On-demand computing is an enterprise-level model of technology by which a customer can purchase cloud services as and when needed.

For example, if a customer needs to utilise additional servers for the duration of a project, they can do so and then drop back to the previous level after the project is completed.

On-demand self service refers to the service provided by cloud computing vendors that enables the provision of cloud resources on demand whenever they are required. In on-demand self service,the user accesses cloud services through an online control panel.

8. How IoT and WoT are related? **(NCERT)**

Ans. **Internet of Things (IOT)** allows us to interact with different devices through Internet with the help of smartphones or computers. But to interact with 'n' number of different devices, we need to install 'n' different apps.

Web of Things (WoT) allows the use of web services to connect anything in the physical world, besides human identities on web.

IoT along with WoT helps to create smart homes, smart offices, smart cities and so on.

9. What are the types of immersive experience?

Ans. There are two types of immersive experiences, which are as follows

  (i) One being when you are actually in a physical environment.

  (ii) The other type of experience is where you are shown around a real or imagined environment *via* desktop, tablet, mobile or *via* VR (Virtual Reality) headset.

10. Write some uses of Virtual Reality.

Ans. There are some uses of Virtual Reality, which are as follows

  (i) In military
  (ii) In sport
  (iii) In mental Health
  (iv) In medical Training
  (v) In education
  (vi) In fashion

11. List some of the applications of Augmented Reality.

Ans. There are few applications of Augmented Reality, which are as follows

  (i) **In Surgery** Augmented Reality and the healthcare industry seem like the perfect match. Complicated medical procedures could be massively improved using AR technology.

  (ii) **In Engineering** Production and manufacturing have been disrupted by innovative technology. Augmented Reality has provided another tool for the creation and maintenance of complicated and expensive machines, making it easier for engineers to carry out repairs.

  (iii) **In Military** Despite seeming like a relatively new application of Augmented Reality, the first fully functioning. AR system was developed at the US Air Force Research Laboratory back in 1992.

12. What are the disadvantages of smart city?

Ans. There are some disadvantages of smart city as

  (i) Lack of public awareness and social responsibility.

  (ii) Building and maintaining the infrastructure is costly and challenging.

  (iii) Demands 24×7 connectivity and power supply.

  (iv) Security issues in terms of public data.

  (v) May lead a way towards social discrimination.

13. How are robots helpful in our daily life and industries?

Ans. They are used routinely to carry out many tasks that people don't want to do because such jobs are boring, dirty or dangerous. Robots can also be programmed to carry out some tasks that are too complex for humans. Robots most obviously impact everyday life in the service capacity. In households, robots, like cooking bots, lawn-mower and vacuum bots ease jobs.

Industrial robots have helped to boost productivity, safety and time savings. Robots are able to produce incredibly accurate, consistent and high quality work without needing breaks or holidays off. Industrial robots also help to remove workers from the hazardous environments and back breaking labor.

• Long Answer Type Questions

14. Explain the term big data. Also, explain its characteristics.

Ans. The generation of data sets of enormous volume and complexity called Big Data. Big data is a term that describes the large volume of data – both structured and unstructured – that inundates a business on a day-to-day basis. Big data can be analysed for insights that lead to better decisions and strategic business moves.

The characteristics of big data are as follows

  (i) **Volume** The most prominent characteristic of big data is its enormous size. If a particular data set is of such large size that it is difficult to process it with traditional DBMS tools, it can be termed as big data.

  (ii) **Velocity** It represents the rate at which the data under consideration is being generated and stored. Big data has an exponentially higher rate of generation than traditional data sets.

  (iii) **Variety** It asserts that a data set has varied data, such as structured, semi-structured and unstructured data. Some examples are text, images, videos, web pages and so on.

  (iv) **Veracity** Big data can be sometimes inconsistent, biased, and noisy or there can be abnormality in the data or issues with the data collection methods. Veracity refers to the trustworthiness of the data because processing such incorrect data can give wrong results or mislead the interpretations.

  (iv) **Value** Big data is not only just a big pile of data, but also possess to have hidden patterns and useful knowledge which can be of high business value.

15. Explain cloud computing in detail and also specifying its types.

Ans. Cloud computing is the delivery of computing services including servers, storage, databases, networking, software, analytics, and intelligence over the Internet to offer faster innovation, flexible resources and economies of scale. You typically pay only for cloud services you use, helping lower your operating costs, run your infrastructure more efficiently and scale as your business needs change.

There are three types of cloud deployments categorized based on an organization's ability to manage and secure assets as follows

(i) **Public Cloud** It is managed by third party which provides cloud services over the Internet to public. They offer solutions for minimizing IT infrastructure costs and act as a good option for handling peak loads on the local infrastructure. A public cloud is meant to serve multiple users, not a single customer.

(ii) **Private Cloud** It is distributed system that works on a private infrastructure and providing the users with dynamic provisioning of computing resources.

(iii) **Hybrid Cloud** It is a heterogeneous distributed system resulted by combining facilities of public cloud and private cloud. For this reason, they are also called heterogeneous clouds.

16. Explain artificial intelligence along with their applications.

Ans. Artificial intelligence is the simulation of human intelligence processes by machines, especially computer systems. Specific applications of AI include expert systems, natural language processing, speech recognition and machine vision.

The intelligence demonstrated by machines is known as artificial intelligence. Artificial intelligence has grown to be very popular in today's world. It is the simulation of natural intelligence in machines that are programmed to learn and mimic the actions of humans.

These machines are able to learn with experience and perform human-like tasks. As technologies such as AI continue to grow, they will have a great impact on our quality of life. It's natural but everyone today wants to connect with AI technology somehow, may it be as an end-user or pursuing a career in artificial intelligence.

Some applications of artificial intelligence are as follows

(i) **Administration** AI systems are helping with the routine, day-to-day administrative tasks to minimise human errors and maximise efficiency. Transcriptions of medical notes through NLP and helps structure patient information to make it easier for doctors to read it.

(ii) **Telemedicine** For non-emergency situations, patients can reach out to a hospital's AI system to analyse their symptoms, input their vital signs and assess if there's a need for medical attention. This reduces the workload of medical professionals by bringing only crucial cases to them.

(iii) **Assisted Diagnosis** Through computer vision and convolutional neural networks, AI is now capable of reading MRI scans to check for tumours and other malignant growths, at an exponentially faster pace than radiologists can, with a considerably lower margin of error.

(iv) **Robot-assisted Surgery** Robotic surgeries have a very minuscule margin-of-error and can consistently perform surgeries round-the-clock without getting exhausted. Since they operate with such a high degree of accuracy, they are less invasive than traditional methods, which potentially reduces the time patients spend in the hospital recovering.

(v) **Vital Stats Monitoring** A person's state of health is an ongoing process, depending on the varying levels of their respective vitals stats. With wearable devices achieving mass-market popularity now, this data is not available on tap, just waiting to be analysed to deliver actionable insights. Since vital signs have the potential to predict health fluctuations even before the patient is aware, there are a lot of live-saving applications here.

17. What is Machine Learning?

Ans. **Machine Learning (ML)** is a type of Artificial Intelligence (AI) that allows software applications to become more accurate at predicting outcomes without being explicitly programmed to do so.

Machine learning algorithms use historical data as input to predict new output values.

Recommendation engines are a common use case for machine learning. Other popular uses include fraud detection, spam filtering, malware threat detection, business process automation (BPA) and predictive maintenance.

Machine learning is important because it gives enterprises a view of trends in customer behavior and business operational patterns, as well as supports the development of new products. Many of today's leading companies, such as Facebook, Google and Uber, make machine learning a central part of their operations. Machine learning has become a significant competitive differentiator for many companies.

Classical machine learning is often categorised by how an algorithm learns to become more accurate in its predictions. There are four basic approaches

(i) Supervised learing

(ii) Unsupervised learing

(iii) Semi-supervised learning

(iv) Reinforcement learing

18. Differentiate cloud computing and grid computing.

Ans. Differences between cloud computing and grid computing are

Cloud computing	Grid computing
Cloud computing follows client-server computing architecture.	Grid computing follows a distributed computing architecture.
Scalability is high.	Scalability is normal.
Cloud computing is more flexible than grid computing.	Grid computing is less flexible than cloud computing.
Cloud operates as a centralised management system.	Grid operates as a decentralised management system.

19. Write in short on how Grid computing can help process jobs better. Also compare the advantages and disadvantages of it.

Ans. The major benefit of computer grids over single supercomputers lies in their flexibility and computing power. Using a computer grid for large amounts of data is more efficient than doing so on a single, memory-hungry supercomputer. It is also more reliable due to reduced downtime risks and is considerably less expensive.

Grid computing is a data processing choice for large companies and academic institutes. It is efficient, affordable and fast while delivering high levels of accuracy and data integrity. Computer grids can involve risks, but, as mentioned earlier, check and balance measures can greatly mitigate them.

In short, computer grids are one of the most attractive and cost-effective means of getting massive computing loads processed. And it's an area of computing technology that is growing fast as data loads increase exponentially across many industries.

Advantages of Grid Computing

  (i) They are not that expensive.
 (ii) They are quite efficient and reliable machines and can solve complex problem in limited time.
(iii) They are scalable.
 (iv) Grid Computing follows distributed computing architecture.
  (v) Grid Computing is application oriented.
 (vi) They work in a decentralized management system.
(vii) They can use existing hardware.
(viii) Can easily associate with other organization.
 (ix) Tasks and instructions can be performed in parallel speeding.
  (x) Grid computing works in a group if any one of the computer is unavailable the workload is distributed across the remaining computers.
 (xi) The grid computing can be upgrade on the fly without scheduling downtime.

Disadvantages of Grid Computing

  (i) They are not interactive for job submissions.
 (ii) Grid system is not fully evolved.
(iii) Difficult in sharing resources across different admins.
 (iv) Grid environment can work with smaller servers.
  (v) Some Application may not work with full potential.

20. How does Natural Language Processing work? Write few of its practical applications.

Ans. It's an intuitive behaviour used to convey information and meaning with semantic cues such as words, signs or images. While the terms AI and NLP might conjure images of futuristic robots, there are already basic examples of NLP at work in our daily lives.

In natural language processing, human language is separated into fragments so that the grammatical structure of sentences and the meaning of words can be analyzed and understood in context. This helps computers read and understand spoken or written text in the same way as humans.

NLP combines computational linguistics-rule-based modeling of human language—with statistical, machine learning and deep learning models. NLP drives computer programs that translate text from one language to another, respond to spoken commands and summarize large volumes of text rapidly—even in real time.

Practical Applications

  (i) **Search Autocorrect and Autocomplete** Whenever you search for something on Google, after typing 2-3 letters, it shows you the possible search terms. It's a wonderful application of natural language processing and a great example of how it is affecting millions around the world, including you and me. Search autocomplete and autocorrect both help us in finding accurate results much efficiently.

 (ii) **Language Translator** It translates a piece of text in one language to another .The technique behind it is Machine Translation.

Machine Translation is the procedure of automatically converting the text in one language to another language while keeping the meaning intact. Due to evolution in the field of neural networks, availability of humongous data and powerful machines, machine translation has become fairly accurate in converting the text from one language to another.

Today, tools like Google Translate can easily convert text from one language to another language. These tools are helping numerous people and businesses in breaking the language barrier and becoming successful.

(iii) **Social Media Monitoring** More and more people these days have started using social media for posting their thoughts about a particular product, policy or matter. These could contain some useful information about an individual's likes and dislikes. Hence analyzing this unstructured data can help in generating valuable insights. Natural Language Processing comes to rescue here too.

Today, various NLP techniques are used by companies to analyze social media posts and know what customers think about their products.

 (iv) **Chatbots** Customer service and experience are the most important thing for any company. It can help the companies improve their products and also keep the customers satisfied. But interacting with every customer manually, and resolving the problems can be a tedious task. This is where Chatbots come into the picture. Chatbots help the companies in achieving the goal of smooth customer experience.

Chapter Test

Multiple Choice Questions

1. .... allows users to have access to their digital resources from any part of the world.
   (a) Phone
   (b) Tablet
   (c) Computer
   (d) Cloud computing

2. Google drive is a .... area in the cloud.
   (a) personal
   (b) special
   (c) public
   (d) None of these

3. SaaS stands for
   (a) System as a Service
   (b) Synchronisation as a Service
   (c) Software as a Service
   (d) None of these

4. .... is an application area of voice / speech recognition.
   (a) Playing back simple information
   (b) Call steering
   (c) Automated identification of caller
   (d) All of these

5. In cloud computing , the cloud means
   (a) a world of computers/ devices on a network that store and supply information to clients
   (b) computing in a local network
   (c) computing at high speed
   (d) computing in a metropolitan area network

Short Answer Type Questions

6. Write some disadvantages of robots.

7. Justify the following statement-
   'Storage of data is cost-effective and time-saving in cloud computing.' **(NCERT)**

8. Five friends plan to try a startup. However, they have a limited budget and limited computer infrastructure. How can they avail the benefits of cloud services to launch their startup? **(NCERT)**

9. Write the use of virtual reality in gaming.

Long Answer Type Questions

10. Write some advantages of robots .

11. Explain the practical usage of big data in various industries .Also, list names of such fields where they are used.

12. What is your view on PaaS ? Write few examples of PaaS.

13. Explain the sensor component of IoT system.

14. Compare advantages and disadvantages of smart cities.

Answers

Multiple Choice Questions

   1. (d)   *2. (a)*   *3. (c)*   *4. (d)*   *5. (a)*

For Detailed Solutions

Scan the code

Practice Paper 1*
(Solved)

General Instructions

- **Time :** 2 Hours
- **Max. Marks :** 35

1. There are 9 questions in the question paper. All questions are compulsory.
2. Question no. 1 is a Case Based Question, which has five MCQs. Each question carries one mark.
3. Question no. 2-6 are Short Answer Type Questions. Each question carries 3 marks.
4. Question no. 7-9 are Long Answer Type Questions. Each question carries 5 marks.
5. There is no overall choice. However, internal choices have been provided in some questions. Students have to attempt only one of the alternatives in such questions.

** As exact Blue-print and Pattern for CBSE Term II exams is not released yet. So the pattern of this paper is designed by the author on the basis of trend of past CBSE Papers. Students are advised not to consider the pattern of this paper as official, it is just for practice purpose.*

1. Direction *Read the case and answers the following questions.*

Mr. Akashdeep wants to work with databases and DBMS softwares. He has started exploring different DBMS/RDBMS softwares. He is also going through the SQL commands that will help him working with the DBMS software. In his course of study he has gone through the concepts of Database, DBMS, Relation, Key fields, Degree, Cardinality etc. He has learnt the commands, Create, Use, Alter, Select, Update etc. To smoothen his concepts help him in solving the following queries.

(i) The ALTER command belongs to the category

    (a) DDL   (b) DML

    (c) TCL   (d) DCL

(ii) The MODIFY clause of ALTER command allows to change

    (a) size of column   (b) type of column

    (c) name of column   (d) Both (a) and (b)

(iii) The data type for a column that will store prices, if items in decimal form can be of type

    (a) float   (b) double

    (c) Both (a) and (b)   (d) varchar

(iv) The data type that does not require a size to be specified is

    (a) float   (b) varchar

    (c) char   (d) date

(v) The format for time in MySQL is

    (a) MM:HH:SS   (b) HH:MM:SS

    (c) SS:MM:HH   (d) SS:DD:HH

2. What do you mean by an operator? Name any four operators used in queries.

Or Write the queries for the following questions using the table Item with the following fields.

(Item_Code, Item_Name, Quantity, Price)

(i) Display the price 500 of item having code as I06.

(ii) Display the name of all items with quantity greater than 50 and price less than 500.

3. Read the following data

Table : ITEM

Item_Code	Item_Name	Price
100	Refrigerator	9000
101	Television	8000
102	Computer	12000
103	Washing Machine	7000

Write MySQL queries for the following (table name is PRODUCT).

(i) Display the details of products whose price is more than 8000 arranged by Item_Name in ascending order.

(ii) Increase the price of the item Television by 10%.

Or (i) Add a new column DtMfg of type date to store the date of manufacture of the products.

(ii) Increase the width of Item_Name column to varchar(50)

4. Consider the following table with their fields.

```
EMPLOYEE(ECODE,ENAME,DESIG,SALARY, DOJ)
```

(i) List the names, salary, PF, HRA, DA of all the employees in the EMPLOYEE Table. HRA is 25% of salary, DA is 10% of salary and PF is 5% of salary. The result should be in descending order of ENAMES.

(ii) Using IN clause display details of employees whose designations are "Manager" or "Officer".

Or Write the syntax of SQL commands with description.

5. Write few uses of Natural Language Processing.

6. Write the uses of immersive experiences in artificial intelligence?

7. Write the situations where you will use the IN, BETWEEN and LIKE clauses.

Or Write the SQL commands for the questions from (i) to (v) on the basis of table Employee.

Emp_no	E_name	Profile	Manager	Hire_date	Salary	Commission	Dept_no
8369	SMITH	CLERK	8902	1990-12-18	8000	NULL	20
8499	ANYA	SALESMAN	8698	1991-02-20	16000	300.00	30
8521	SETH	SALESMAN	8698	1991-02-22	12500	500.00	30
8566	MAHADEVAN	MANAGER	8839	1991-04-02	29850	NULL	20
8654	MOMIN	SALESMAN	8698	1991-09-28	12500	1400.00	30
8698	BINA	MANAGER	8839	1991-05-01	28500	NULL	30
8882	SHIVANSH	MANAGER	8839	1991-06-09	24500	NULL	10
8888	SCOTT	ANALYST	8566	1992-12-09	30000	NULL	20
8839	AMIR	PRESIDENT	NULL	1991-11-18	50000	NULL	10
8844	KULDEEP	SALESMAN	8698	1991-09-08	15000	0.00	30

(i) Display Employee Name and Salary of those employees whose salary is greater than or equal to 22000?

(ii) Display details of empolyees those are not getting commission.

(iii) Display employee name and salary of those employees who have their salary in range of 2000 to 4000?

(iv) Display the name, profile and salary of employee(s) who doesn't have manager?

(v) Display the name of employee whose name contains "A" as fourth alphabet.

8. Consider the table STUDENT given below and write answer for (i) and SQL commands for (ii) to (v).

Student_No	Class	Name	Game	G_Grade	Section	Marks
01	7	Rahul	Swimming	B	A	99
02	8	Sameer	Tenis	A	B	20
03	10	Dushyant	FootBall	C	C	87
04	12	Kapil	Tennis	D	C	90
05	6	Ravinder	Cricket	A	B	97

(i) What is the degree and cardinality of the table.

(ii) Display Student_No and G_Grade of all students from table STUDENT.

(iii) List the Name from table STUDENT whose Student_No is 04 or 05 or 02.

(iv) Display Game and Marks for those students whose name started with an alphabet 'D'.

(v) Write a query to display Name and Section for those students whose Marks lies between 85 to 100.

Or Explain grid computing along with its categories.

9. What are constraints of a table? Name them all. Discuss UNIQUE, CHECK and DEFAULT constraints.

Or Write SQL queries with respect to the table cellphone given below

Table : Cellphone

Modelld	Brand	Type	Cost
M01	Samsung	4G	12500
C11	Realme	2G	15000
T12	TCL	3G	7000
D402	Nokia	4G	6500
M02	Samsung	5G	2500

(i) To display details of 4G cellphones whose cost is greater than 10000.

(ii) To increase cost of 5G phones by 20%.

(iii) To add a new column DateofMfg of type Date.

(iv) To display ModelId and cost of Samsung phones.

(v) To display details of phones whose ModelId ends with "2".

Explanations

1. (i) (*a*) The ALTER command that makes changes to the structure of a table belongs to the DDL category.
   (ii) (*d*) The ALTER command's MODIFY clause allows to change both a column's size and data type.
   (iii) (*c*) Since the price column will store data with decimal values it can be of type float or double.
   (iv) (*d*) Since for date data type the number characters are fixed, that is YYYY-MM-DD, it does not require size to be specified.
   (v) (*b*) The format for time is Hour : Minute : Second.

2. An operator is a component of an expression that represents the action that should be taken over a set of values. Four operators used in queries are
   (i) Arithmetic operators
   (ii) Comparison operators
   (iii) Boolean/Logical operator
   (iv) Between operator

Or

```
(i) mysql>SELECT Price FROM Item
           WHERE Item_Code = 'I06';
(ii) mysql>SELECT Item_Name
           FROM Item
           WHERE (Quantity >  50) AND
           (Price < 500);
```

3. ```
   (i) Select * from ITEM where Price > 8000
       order by Item_Name ;
   (ii) Update ITEM set price = price
        +price*10/100 where
        Item_Name="Television";
   ```

<p align="center">*Or*</p>

```
(i) Alter table ITEM ADD DtMfg Date;
(ii) Alter table ITEM MODIFY Item_Name
     varchar(50);
```

4. ```
   (i) Select ENAME,SALARY,SALARY *0.05 as
       "PF", SALARY *0.25 as "HRA", SALARY
       *0.10 as "DA" from EMPLOYEE order by
       ENAME DESC;
   (ii) Select * from EMPLOYEE where DESIG
        IN("Manager" ,"Officer");
   ```

Or

SQL is followed by a unique set of rules and guidelines called syntax.

Symbols Used in Syntax of SQL Statements

Symbol	Description
|	Symbolic way of 'or' whatever precedes this symbol may optionally be replaced by whatever follows it.
[ ]	Everything enclosed in it is optional.
...	Whatever precedes, it may be repeated number of times.
.,..	Whatever precedes, it may be repeated number of times with individual occurrences of commas.
{ }	Everything enclosed in it, is evaluating different symbols (1., ... etc.).
< >	SQL and some other terms are enclosed by this angle brackets.

5. Following are the uses of Natural Language Processing:
   (i) Sentiment Analysis.
   (ii) Text Classification.
   (iii) Chatbots & Virtual Assistants.
   (iv) Text Extraction.
   (v) Machine Translation.
   (vi) Text Summarisation.
   (vii) Market Intelligence.
   (viii) Auto-correct.

6. With the three dimensional (3D) videography, the joy of watching movies in theatres has reached to a new level. Video games are also being developed to provide immersive experiences to the player. Immersive experience allows us to visualise, feel and react by stimulating over senses. It enhances our interaction and involvement, making them more realistic and engaging. Immersive experiences have been used in the field of training such as driving simulators, flight simulator and so on.

7. **The IN** clause is used in place of multiple OR clauses. The IN clause can replace multiple Ors joining the conditions in a query. This makes the command smaller.

   e.g. To display the employee details for employees working in departments "Sales","Purc" and "IT" the command with and without IN will be :

   Select * from Employee where dept="Sales" or dept="Purc" or dept="IT";

   Select * from Employee where dept IN ("Sales", "Purc","IT");

   The BETWEEN clause is used to match ranges in a query. The >= and <= ranges can be matched using the BETWEEN clause.

   e.g. To display the details of employees getting salary between 50000 and 90000, the command with and without the BETWEEN clause will be

   Select * from Employee where salary>=50000 and salary <=90000;

   Select * from Employee where salary BETWEEN 50000 and 90000;

   The LIKE clause is used in places where a pattern is to be matched in a query, that is where partial information about the match is provided. It uses two wild cards * and _ to match missing characters.

e.g.

(i) To display the details of employees whose name begins with "S" the command will be :

Select * from Employee where name like "S%";

e.g.

(ii) To display details of employees whose department ends with "S" the command will be :

Select * from Employee where dept like "%S";

Or

(i) ```
mysql>SELECT E_name, Salary From
Emloyee WHERE Salary>=22000;
```

(ii) ```
mysql>SELECT * FROM Employee WHERE
Commission IS NULL;
```

(iii) ```
mysql>SELECT E_name, Salary FROM
Employee WHERE Salary BETWEEN 2000 AND
4000;
```

(iv) ```
mysql>SELECT E_name, Profile, Salary
FROM Employee WHERE Manager IS NULL;
```

(v) ```
mysql>SELECT E_name FROM Employee
WHERE E_name LIKE '……… A%';
```

8. (i) **Degree** 7(Degree is the total number of columns)
**Cardinality** 5 (Cardinality is the total number of rows).

(ii) ```
mysql>SELECT Student_No, G_Grade FROM
STUDENT;
```

(iii) ```
mysql>SELECT Name FROM STUDENT WHERE
STUDENT_No IN (04, 05, 02);
```

(iv) ```
mysql>SELECT Game, Marks FROM STUDENT
WHERE Name LIKE 'D%';
```

(v) ```
mysql>SELECT Name, Section FROM
STUDENT WHERE Marks BETWEEN 85 AND
100;
```

*Or*

**Grid computing** is a distributed architecture of large number of computers connected to solve a complex problem. It is a group of networked computers which work together as a virtual super computer to perform large tasks, such as analysing huge sets of data or weather modeling.

Through the cloud, you can assemble and use vast computer grids for specific time periods and purposes, paying if necessary, only for what you use to save both the time and expense of purchasing and deploying the necessary resources yourself.

Unlike parallel computing, grid computing projects typically have no time dependence associated with them. They use computers which are part of the grid only when idle and operators can perform tasks unrelated to the grid at any time.

Grid operations are generally classified into two categories

(i) **Data Grid** A system that handles large distributed data sets used for data management and controlled user sharing.

(ii) **CPU or Processor Grid** CPU or processor grid system, where processing is moved from one PC to another as needed or a large task is divided into subtasks, and allotted to various nodes for parallel processing.

9. Constraints are checks or conditions given on fields of a table. This restricts entry of invalid data by the database users. Constraints also allow enforcement of business rules into tables. The constraints can be applied on table columns : Primary Key, Foreign Key, Check, Unique, Default.

(i) **Unique Constraint** This constraint ensures that a column or a group of columns in each row have a unique value.

(ii) **Check Constraint** This constraint enforce the domain integrity by limiting the values that are accepted by a column.

(iii) **Default Constraint** This constraint is used to insert a default value into a column that is left blank at the time of input data.

*Or*

(i) ```
Select * from cellphone where
Type="4G" and cost>10000;
```

(ii) ```
Update cellphone set Cost=Cost +
Cost*0.2 where type="5G";
```

(iii) ```
Alter table cellphone ADD DateofMfg
Date;
```

(iv) ```
Select ModelId, Cost from Cellphone
where Brand="Samsung";
```

(v) ```
Select * from cellphone where ModelId
like "%2";
```

Practice Paper 2*
(Unsolved)

General Instructions

■ **Time :** 2 Hours
■ **Max. Marks :** 35

1. There are 9 questions in the question paper. All questions are compulsory.
2. Question no. 1 is a Case Based Question, which has five MCQs. Each question carries one mark.
3. Question no. 2-6 are Short Answer Type Questions. Each question carries 3 marks.
4. Question no. 7-9 are Long Answer Type Questions. Each question carries 5 marks.
5. There is no overall choice. However, internal choices have been provided in some questions. Students have to attempt only one of the alternatives in such questions.

** As exact Blue-print and Pattern for CBSE Term II exams is not released yet. So the pattern of this paper is designed by the author on the basis of trend of past CBSE Papers. Students are advised not to consider the pattern of this paper as official, it is just for practice purpose.*

1. Direction *Read the case and answer the following questions.*

Ravi has recently studied about the basic database concepts. He has come across the terms like database, tables, degree of a table, cardinality of a table, primary key, candidate key, alternate key, etc. He has also learnt that while creating a table, certain constraints may be applied to restrict data in tables and to impose business rules in them .He wants to be more confident about these concepts. Help him by solving the following questions .

(i) If a table "Electronics" has 12 attributes and 10 tuples , the degree of the table is
   (a) 12   (b) 10
   (c) 120   (d) 22

(ii) The header of a table is used in counting the
   (a) degree   (b) cardinality
   (c) candidate key count   (d) None of these

(iii) If a table has 3 columns carrying NOT NULL and UNIQUE values, the maximum number of candidate keys can be
   (a) 2   (b) 3   (c) 1   (d) 0

(iv) Constraints in a table can be added,
   (a) while creating table   (b) after creation of table
   (c) Both (a) and (b)   (d) None of these

(v) Which of the following equation relates primary key, candidate key and alternate key?
   (a) Primary key = Candidate key + Alternate key
   (b) Candidate key = Primary key + Alternate key
   (c) Aternate key = Candidate key – Primary key
   (d) Both (b) and (c)

2. Write some uses of sensors .Explain the sensor components of IoT system.

Or Write MySQL command to create the table STOCK including its constraints. What will the constraint primary Key do?

Table : STOCK

Name_of_Column	Type	Size	Constraint
ID	Decimal	4	Primary Key
Name	Varchar	20	Null
Company	Varchar	20	Null
Price	Decimal	8	Not Null

3. Write in short about fields where virtual reality technology can be applied?

Or Write a command to create the table PAYMENT given below as per the instance chart . What will the Not Null constraint do?

Table : PAYMENT

Field_Name	Type	Size	Constraint
Loan_Number	Integer	4	Primary Key
Payment_Number	Varchar	3	Null
Payment_Date	Date		Null
Payment_Amount	Integer	8	Not Null

4. Which column can be the primary key of the table? What will be the output of the following queries on the basis of EMPLOYEE table?

Table : EMPLOYEE

Emp_Id	Name	Salary
E01	Siya	54000
E02	Joy	NULL
E03	Allena	32000
E04	Neev	42000

(i) `SELECT Salary + 100 FROM EMPLOYEE`
   `WHERE Emp_Id = 'E02';`

(ii) `SELECT Name FROM EMPLOYEE`
   `WHERE Emp_Id = 'E04';`

Or Explain how grid computing can be used in solving a complex problem.

5. What is the use of AS keyword with SELECT statement?

6. Consider the table CUSTOMER

C_ID	C_Name	C_City	C_Salary
100	DUSHYANT	MEERUT	15000
101	RAJ	DELHI	12000
102	VIKAS	GOA	10000

(i) Write a MySQL query to display the names of all customers from Meerut.

(ii) Name the data type used for C_City field.

7. Write the syntax for the following SQL commands
   (i) Drop a database
   (ii) Select a database
   (iii) Insert a new row
   (iv) Update a NULL value
   (v) Change the data type of a column
   (vi) Create a table
   (vii) Drop a table
   (viii) Update a table

Or Write SQL commands for the table Garments.

Table : Garments

GID	Gname	Qty	Price	Type
G01	Trouser	15	775.50	Cotton
G02	Shirt	25	256.55	Cotton
G03	Saree	28	3000.00	Silk
G04	Tie	54	1500.00	Nylon
G05	Handkerchief	65	50.00	Cotton

   (i) Display details of "Cotton" and "Silk" garments.
   (ii) Increase price of "Silk" garments by 200 , if their price is less than 2000.
   (iii) Add a new column Reorder of type integer(4).
   (iv) Remove the column Reorder.
   (v) Delete the records of garments whose Gname has first character as "S" and third character as "r".

8. Find errors in the following SQL statements.
   (i) `SELECT*FROM Student WHERE Name IS = "Amit";`
   (ii) `SELECT*FROM Employee WHERE Salary BETWEEN 1000, 2000;`
   (iii) `SELECT*FROM Employee WHERE Name = "A%";`
   (iv) `SELECT Name,Subject FROM Student WHERE Average >20 and < 30;`
   (v) `SELECT*FROM Student WHERE Name = "Amit" AND Name ="Sumit";`

Or Write commands required for the following cases.
   (i) To add a new record
   (ii) To increase a value in an existing record
   (iii) To remove a table with all its data
   (iv) To modify an existing column of table
   (v) To remove a column of a table

9. Explain the uses and characteristics of cloud computing.

Or Describe Internet of Things (IoT) and its advantages.

Answers

1. *(i) (a)*   *(ii) (d)*   *(iii) (b)*   *(iv) (c)*   *(v) (d)*

Practice Paper 3*
(Unsolved)

General Instructions

■ Time : 2 Hours
■ Max. Marks : 35

1. There are 9 questions in the question paper. All questions are compulsory.
2. Question no. 1 is a Case Based Question, which has five MCQs. Each question carries one mark.
3. Question no. 2-6 are Short Answer Type Questions. Each question carries 3 marks.
4. Question no. 7-9 are Long Answer Type Questions. Each question carries 5 marks.
5. There is no overall choice. However, internal choices have been provided in some questions. Students have to attempt only one of the alternatives in such questions.

As exact Blue-print and Pattern for CBSE Term II exams is not released yet. So the pattern of this paper is designed by the author on the basis of trend of past CBSE Papers. Students are advised not to consider the pattern of this paper as official, it is just for practice purpose.

1. **Direction** *Read the case and answer the following questions.*

   Rahul , a database user is recently going through SQL commands on data manipulation. He found that the commands come under the category of DML – Data Manipulation Language. The understood that these commands mostly work with data of the table. The commands under DML allow to add , modify , delete and view data. The command insert into helps to add records to a table. The Select command displays or searches data from tables . The Update command helps him in modifying the data of the table and the Delete command removes records from a table. On the basis of his above study he has to solve the following assignment. Help him in his assignment.

   (i) Rahul wants an alternative to the $>=$ and $<=$ operators. He can use
      (a) Like   (b) Order By   (c) Between   (d) NULL

   (ii) Using a single update command, how many tables can he update?
      (a) 2   (b) 3   (c) 1   (d) 4

   (iii) The clause he has to use with Order By to arrange data in descending order is
      (a) DESC   (b) DES
      (c) Descending   (d) Both (a) and (c)

   (iv) The delete command can be used to delete ……… number of records.
      (a) 1   (b) 2   (c) 3   (d) any number

   (v) He used the command : "Insert values INTO emp(1,"Jack","Sales",45000);" , but the command did not work. What will be the correct command.
      (a) Insert into emp values(1,"Jack","Sales",45000);
      (b) Insert into emp values(1,Jack,Sales,45000);
      (c) Insert into emp values(1,'Jack','Sales',45000);
      (d) Both (a) and (c)

2. Explain the use of Update command. Also give two example commands where the update command can be used to conditionally update a table using single condition and using multiple conditions.

Or How will you make changes to the structure of a table? Write the command and also write two example commands (i) To add a column to a table, (ii) To rename a column.

3. How can Immersive experiences be used in Military and other training sessions? Give examples of two other real life uses of Immersive experiences.

Or Write the properties of a Smart city. Do you find any disadvantages of a Smart City? List any two.

4. Write SQL queries with respect to the table Hostel given below

Table : Hostel

HostelNo	HostelName	Location	Charges
H1	South	Delhi	3450
H2	North	Mumbai	7650
H3	East	Bangalore	9000
H4	West	Chennai	5600
H5	South West	Kolkata	7600

(i) Display names and locations of hostels outside "Kolkata".

(ii) Increase charges of Hostels in Chennai and Mumbai.

(iii) Add a new column State varchar(25) to store the statename to which they belong to.

Or With respect to the above table Hostel , write queries for the following

(i) To add the following record to the table
(H6,"North-West","Dehradun",8000)

(ii) To change width of the column HostelName to varchar(40).

(iii) To rename the column charges to Hostelcharges.

5. State and explain the command that opens a database for working.

6. Distinguish between UPDATE and ALTER commands.

7. Write SQL queries with respect to the table Car given below

Table : Car

CarNo	Model	Make	Price
WB780	Calistro180	Maruti	560000
MU879	Roadking500	Hyundai	750000
CH123	Rolls200	Hyundai	200000
DL890	Suzuki800	Tata	350000
CH345	Rivero250	Tata	400000

(i) Display Model, Price of Hyundai cars.

(ii) Display only CarNo of cars whose price is between 400000 and 600000.

(iii) To add a new column Grade char(10) to store the grade of the car.

(iv) To display details of cars whose model name has "II" somewhere in between.

(v) To display remove the column Make.

Or Write SQL queries with respect to the table Car given above

(i) Insert a new record (WB678,Hindustan100,HindMotor,450000) to the table.

(ii) Display details of cars who have "CH" in their Carno , in ascending order of price.

(iii) Display the structure of the table.

(iv) Display Model, Make and Price of all cars whose price is above 700000 in descending order of price.

(v) Decrease price of cars by 15%, if their price is above 700000 and their Make is "Hyundai".

8. Write SQL queries with respect to the table Accessories given below

Table : Accessories

No	Name	Price	ID
A01	Mother Board	12000	S01
A02	Hard Disk	5000	S01
A03	Keyboard	500	S02
A04	Mouse	300	S01
A05	Mother Board	13000	S02
A06	Keyboard	400	S03
A07	LCD	6000	S04
A08	LCD	5500	S05
A09	Mouse	350	S05

(i) To display Name and Price of all the Accessories in ascending order of their Price.

(ii) To create the above table with appropriate data types.

(iii) To remove the records of accessories whose name starts with "M".

(iv) To display the details of all accessories in descending order of Name whose name has "Board" at its end.

(v) To add the last record to the table.

Or Write SQL queries with respect to the table Accessories given above

(i) Add a column Mfgname of type varchar(30) to store the manufacturer name.

(ii) To display all accessories whose price falls between 200 and 1500 in descending order of price.

(iii) To delete the record of "LCD" whose price is above 5700.

(iv) To display the fields, data types, sizes and constraints of the table.

(v) To remove the table Accessories completely.

9. Explain and elaborate the following

(i) Uses of cloud computing services

(ii) Uses of Robots

(iii) Facilities in Smart cities

Or Write a paragraph about each of the following

(i) Characteristics of cloud computing

(ii) SaaS

(iii) Types of cloud deployments.

Answers

1. (i) (c)   (ii) (c)   (iii) (d)   (iv) (d)   (v) (d)

Printed by Libri Plureos GmbH in Hamburg,
Germany